Inspirience

Inspirience

Meditation Unbound

The Unconditioned Path to
Spiritual Awakening

RICHARD L. HAIGHT

Shinkaikan Body, Mind, Spirit LLC
www.richardhaight.net

ISBN 978-0-9992100-1-7

Disclaimer:
1. Some names and identifying details have been changed to protect the privacy of individuals.
2. This book is not intended as a substitute for the medical or psychological advice of physicians or psychiatrists. The reader should regularly consult health practitioner in matters relating to his or her physical or mental/emotional health and particularly with respect to any symptoms that may require diagnosis or medical attention.

Publisher's Cataloging-In-Publication Data
(Prepared by The Donohue Group, Inc.)

Names: Haight, Richard L., 1973-
Title: Inspirience : meditation unbound : the unconditioned path to spiritual awakening / Richard L. Haight.
Description: [Rogue River, Oregon] : Shinkaikan Body, Mind, Spirit LLC, [2017] | Includes bibliographical references.
Identifiers: ISBN 978-0-9992100-1-7 | ISBN 978-0-9992100-3-1 (ebook)
Subjects: LCSH: Meditation. | Transcendence (Philosophy) | Experience. | Spiritual life. | Self-help techniques.
Classification: LCC BL627 .H35 2017 (print) | LCC BL627 (ebook) | DDC 204/.35--dc23

Published by Shinkaikan Body, Mind, Spirit LLC
www.richardhaight.net

Shinkaido penned by Osaki Shizen (July 2012)

CONTENTS

INTRODUCTION

As I begin, I must confess to an ulterior motive. Beyond teaching meditation, beyond all else, it is my goal to free the reader of the voice within that says, "I'm not ready for enlightenment." Consider that every journey begins with a single step. If you take one step right now, then you are well on your way.

There is a presence, intelligence, and power so perfect, so loving that no human words can adequately describe it, and it's within you. With this presence, there is absolutely no judgment or negativity of any sort. There is perfect forgiveness, for there is unconditioned love. Although there is the ability to perceive disharmony, there is no binding, fear, or ignorance, only total harmony and oneness.

This presence is not limited to you, for it is in everyone and everything. It pervades the entire universe. It is so beautiful and vibrantly harmonious that it transcends any possible conjurings of the mind.

When we are in tune with this presence, we realize that there is no other. That all is indivisibly one, and nothing can be done to change that fact. After tuning in with this presence, the desire to share it with the world is only natural, for just as this presence resolves your suffering, so too does it resolve the suffering of the world. But to speak of this presence, we need an indicator, a word. As the words *Tao, Buddha, God,* and so forth have taken on so many extraneous associations over time, I have endeavored to come up with a fresh, undefined word that is as free of baggage as absolutely possible. Because this presence simply *is*, I refer to *it* as Isness. Please be mindful that Isness is only an indicator of something deeper—there is nothing sacred in the word. Even to say that the fundamental presence *is*, is incorrect, for it both *is* and *is not*, is both and neither simultaneously. Under these conditions, the word *Isness* will have to suffice. Many apologies.

Although Isness is at the very core of each individual ever born, it seems only a tiny fraction of people throughout history have had a direct conscious awareness of Isness. The experience is so inspiring, so mystifying, and so heart-opening that most people who have had such an experience are likely to dedicate their lives to the exploration and revelation of it. I am no exception to this formula.

By all accounts, a direct, conscious experience of Isness is awe-inspiring and utterly mind-blowing. As an Isness experience is so drastically different in nature from all other human experience, I have come up with a new word to indicate it: *inspirience*. The root terms of *inspirience* are *inspire* and *experience*.

My main focus in life is assisting other people to tune in to Isness, so that it may begin transforming their lives just as it has mine. Through individuals like you, Isness inspirience will spread like a wildfire, burning away the accumulated deadwood that has been clogging up the flow of life. As the number of inspiriencing individuals increases, truth, integrity, and unconditioned love will come to the fore. Bigotry, hatred, violence, crime, and corruption at all levels of society will fade away. Human beings will live inspired lives filled with a sense of connection and purpose, in communion with all life on Earth.

In the decades since my first Isness inspirience, I have discovered a number of powerful tools that help individuals inspirience Isness. In this book, I will focus primarily on the tool of meditation. My goal is to clearly and concisely demonstrate how meditation can be used as a simple, powerful tool for revealing what is at your very core: Isness.

If you are interested in applying meditation along your path of awakening, then I believe you will appreciate the simple, unique, and highly practical approach taught here. I have endeavored to include my personal exploration of meditation — the successes, the failures, the misunderstandings, the corrections, and the reasoning behind it all. In so doing I hope to expedite your awakening process. Humanity cannot afford too many more dead ends.

Most forms of meditation have Eastern religious practices, such as Buddhism, Taoism, Zen, and Yogic traditions, as their source. But the meditations taught in this book do not come from tradition. They were revealed through my own lifelong, personal exploration of meditation, absent a formal teacher. After an inspirience at age 22, Isness became my teacher, so all that is taught here stems directly from its source, new, and unencumbered by tradition. Any similarity to any other teachings may be an indication of a shared teacher, Isness.

Many forms of meditation have been scientifically proven to provide such health benefits as lowered blood pressure, improved general heart health, stress relief, improved concentration, better memory and overall increased psychological well-being. You will find these very same benefits come from practicing the meditations in this book. Moreover, what is taught here will help you to have tremendous insight, to burn off the inner deadwood, and to realize Isness at the very core of your being. If you practice properly, all of these benefits will be received through your daily life — the true path of awakening.

Saint Paul wrote that your body is the temple, which is to say, your body holds the wisdom that you seek. While there is no way for me to be certain what Paul actually meant by his words, my own awakening process has proven to me that the body does indeed hold the wisdom we seek.

If the body holds hidden wisdom, we will need a way to gain access to that wisdom. The path to that wisdom is your life. The guide on your path is your body, for it does not lie. The body contains an unfathomable amount of untapped information that will ultimately assist you in your awakening as you open up to that hidden wisdom. Meditation is merely a tool to assist you in the process of discovering the wisdom hidden within. The magic is within you, not the meditation.

In this work, I will be using an uncommon set of terms to indicate awakening or enlightenment. For the purposes of instruction, I find the terms *unveiling*, *unbinding*, or *unfolding* to be quite fitting. Unfoldment, for example, makes a good metaphor for awakening. Let's say that whatever truth *is* is a word written in the very deepest place within you, which is represented by the center of a fresh piece of paper. What would happen to the word written there if we were to fold the paper in half? With just one fold we have already lost sight of the word written there. With each additional fold, the truth is further distanced from perception. Although the word is still there, it is, for all intents and purposes, unavailable to us. We may soon forget anything of value was ever written there and begin using that paper frivolously.

Once the individual is aware that a great secret is written there, would it make any sense to continue folding the paper still further? Of course not. To learn of the secret, one would need to undo each and every fold, reversing the folding process that has been obscuring the word. Yes, Isness is at the very core of each individual, but it is deeply obscured.

The words *unveiling* and *unbinding* indicate something that has been covering over truth or boxing it in. With unveiling, for example, we could imagine that truth were like an illuminated light bulb buried in the mud. The light is shining just as brightly as ever, but the mud would require removal before the light could be of service in your life.

Unbinding is probably the most accurate term for the awakening process, but it is also the most elusive to understand. Imagine that the "light" of Isness is the source of consciousness. When consciousness is used incorrectly, it is as if the frequency of that light drops tremendously. The light becomes distorted as it bends around the falsehood to form a disharmony that inhabits the individual and disrupts his or her life. In order to resolve the individual back to harmony, one would need to correct the falsehood that created the original distortion.

Awakening, enlightenment, unfoldment, unveiling, and unbinding are all models that can serve to aid our process. They are good only so long as they serve their intended function, so please be careful not to place too much weight on any of them, lest the words bind you.

If meditation is a tool, your body is the guide, and your life is the path. What are the folds? What are the bindings? Ideas, concepts, ideologies, biases, assumptions, emotional habits, feelings, traumas, addictions, patterns, regrets, lies, fears, phobias, beliefs, and much, much more — everything that you cling to, really. These things constitute the folds, the bindings, of your life that have served to obscure what is at the very center just waiting to be perceived — Isness.

Anything we cling to is a fold. To avoid turning meditation into a fold, we will focus on principle rather than form, for the mind insecurely latches onto form. By focusing on principle, we can get the most out of meditation without binding to the form.

The meditations herein won't tell you what is written on your paper; instead, they will help you to unfold that paper, to unbind your soul, so you can see, or more precisely inspirience, Isness for yourself in your daily life, and in so doing, end your suffering. In this way, quite naturally, you are a light to the world.

PART 1

The Foundations of Meditation

CHAPTER 1

What Is Meditation?

I experienced my first meditation in karate practice at age 12. At the beginning of class the students sat on their knees, in a line. The teacher said, "Meditate," in a stern voice. We closed our eyes in silence for a few minutes before we began our workout. We repeated the same process at the end of class. There was only one problem: I had no idea what the process was. I just sat there for a few minutes, not knowing what to do.

As I matured, I decided to ask what we were supposed to do during "meditation." I was not comfortable asking the teacher, so I asked a senior student instead. After a moment of thought he said, "Well, I visualize the techniques." I decided to follow this advice and visualize techniques too. This continued for many years before I had any further insight into meditation.

At age 16 I began dating a girl who, unbeknownst to me, meditated. One evening, I found her sitting cross-legged with her eyes closed. I asked her what she was doing and without opening her eyes, she said, "I'm meditating." I wondered what her method of meditation was, so I asked. "I sit with spine erect, close my eyes, and then focus on calming my breath," she said. I sat next to her and gave it a try. I was surprised to find this method created a paradoxical state of calm alertness — two qualities I hadn't realized could work in tandem. I decided that I would incorporate this method into my karate practice.

About a month later, my mother and I got into a terrible argument — about what, I can no longer remember. I was so frustrated that I could barely think straight. I stormed out of the house mid-argument and headed up the hillside behind our ranch. The sun was just setting on a warm summer evening. Once I reached the top of the hill, I walked into the sagebrush off the trail and found a little clearing where I could sit comfortably.

I crossed my legs and sat with erect spine, just as I had learned from my girlfriend. I decided that I was going to meditate myself back to calm. I focused my attention on my lower abdomen and tried to control my breathing. With each breath, I intended to calm myself. With each wave of frustration, I reoriented myself toward calm through my breath. After a time, my mind began to slow. My thoughts became clearer and less judgmental. I kept at the calming breath and soon found myself immersed in a very relaxed, inner spaciousness. The negative feelings ceased. The breathing continued almost as if I were being breathed by the universe. It was a strange feeling that I made mental note of. I opened my eyes to find that it was dark outside. I must have been sitting there for almost an hour.

I continued meditating because I so enjoyed the calm spaciousness, though there was no longer any negativity that I could find. It felt right to walk, so I got up and walked for a few minutes before a new location drew my attention. I sat down in a small clearing, just about six feet from a large eucalyptus tree, and resumed my inner journey.

At some point my body felt as if it had become transparent, as if it were no longer separate from the surrounding environment. Shortly thereafter, I felt a pulling sensation on my left side. Without my intending to do so, my head turned, and I looked in the direction of the feeling. There, no more than 30 feet from me, stood a coyote on the trail. It stopped to watch me. Our eyes met, but there was no fear, only calm. The coyote sniffed in my direction for a bit then slowly moved away, into the brush, to resume the evening hunt. My eyes closed again — not a single thought arose.

Sometime later in the evening, I heard the sound of something climbing the tree just in front of me. Again my eyes opened, and I looked up, into the lower branches of the tree, to find a bobcat settling onto its hunting perch, about 15 feet above me. The cat seemed entirely unaware that a human was mere feet away. My eyes closed again. I had not a single residual thought on the topic.

I wish I could say how long the meditation lasted, but time seemed to have disappeared. When it felt right to arise and head back down the hill, I got up without a thought and walked back home in total clarity. Only later did it occur to me how truly amazing that evening was.

Imagine the smell of an angry teen boy on a summer night — ripe, to be sure. Surely, the animals must have smelled me there. That scent must have been all over the hillside, and even more concentrated in the areas where I sat. There was no wind to speak of, so there would have been minimal scent dispersion. Why didn't the coyote run from me? I know that it saw me. My head turned to look at it, and our gazes met. It showed not the slightest concern. Then there was the bobcat that climbed the tree right in front of me. I don't know whether it saw me, but surely it smelled me. Nonetheless, it behaved as if I weren't even there. Why?

There is no way to know what those animals were feeling about me that night, but I can speculate. I suspect that they looked at me and felt a deep calm, and were therefore simply not threatened. I took the animals' reaction to be an indicator that I was doing something right in my meditation. What's more, the angst, frustration, and racing mind that accompanied me up the hill were completely transformed through the process. I felt calm, clear and, well, fantastic on my walk back to the house. With this experience I was sure that my meditation practice was heading in the right direction.

Afterward, I was sure that meditation would be easy for me. The only problem was it seemed that no matter how I tried, I could never get to the same depth again. Meditation became a constant struggle, and little by little meditation sessions became shorter and less frequent until eventually I stopped using this method entirely. The struggle and subsequent discouragement are common among meditators. I knew if I were ever going to make use of meditation, I would have to find a way that was less willful.

There was another issue with the method I was using. It required that I close my eyes. As I was serious about my martial arts training, it struck me as odd that we should close our eyes during meditation. Shouldn't we be able to meditate with our eyes open, I wondered?

CHAPTER 2

Martial Meditation

I made no progress in meditation until some months later, when my martial arts teacher showed me how to develop "internal energy," as he described it, by focusing intention when punching. The idea was to blow out a lit candle by punching at, without actually hitting, the flame. "If your ki is sufficient, the candle will be blown out by your punch," he said. I spent months and months lighting candles for this exercise. It took me several weeks before I could get the candle to blow out from a punch, and several more months before the candle would blow out consistently.

Gradually through practice, I began thinking that it was not "ki" that was blowing out the candle, as I had assumed, but the wind from a very smooth punch. If the arm travels very smoothly and directly toward the candle, the movement will channel the air directly through the flame, blowing it out. Rough or undeveloped punching will only cause the flame to waver. Success, in this case, is not a matter of physical strength, but instead one of accuracy, speed, and smoothness.

But you might wonder what punching has to do with meditation. I noticed when doing this exercise for extended lengths of time that I would go into a sort of meditation, wherein my mind would quiet, feeling clear and calm. I theorized that staring at the candle created this effect, so I discarded candle punching and began candle staring.

I sat in front of a lit candle and stared at it for as long as I could. After a fairly short time, I noticed that my eyes would defocus, with the flickering candle flame occupying the very center of an enlarged visual field. My body relaxed and calmed, while a heightened sense of awareness grew within me. Many years later I learned that candle staring was a secret training method among ninja of ancient Japan to develop awareness.

But there was a problem with this meditation, in my opinion. I didn't like that I had to use candles. It was a practical matter that limited meditation too much; after all, it required having a candle and a lighter. It occurred to me that maybe the crucial point was not so much the candle, but focusing the eyes on a fixed point. I discarded the candle method. Instead of using candles, I began focusing on a spot on the wall. After a few minutes of focusing on one fixed point, my eyes began to defocus, taking in the whole visual field. Calm aliveness indicated that I was heading in the right direction.

Maybe the secret to meditation was not focusing but instead defocusing the eyes, I thought. I got more clarity on this issue by stargazing. Because our family lived on a ranch in the countryside, there were few lights to dampen the celestial view, unlike what city-dwellers face. What a shame it is that so many people have spent most of their lives not knowing the universe extends out into infinity, and all you have to do is look up to see heavenly glory. I lay on the lawn and allowed my eyes to take in the entirety of the night sky. Sometimes the stars stood out so vividly that it felt like I could just reach up and touch one.

As I played with stargazing, I noticed an odd phenomenon. When I focused on a bright star, like

Polaris, I could see it clearly, as well as many dimmer stars, but when I tried to focus on dimmer stars, they faded out of view. I could see the dimmer stars only at the periphery of my visual field. Of course the natural desire when one wishes to see something clearly is to focus on it, but with dim stars, focusing was not feasible — counterintuitive, but true.

Finally I had my answer. When we wish to perceive something subtle, defocusing vision is more effective than focusing. Meditation brings us to a subtler consciousness, so maybe gazing is the secret to meditation as well. I had been using focus techniques to meditate, like staring at a candle or at a fixed point on the wall, but the meditation never really kicked in until the eyes tired and began to defocus.

Realizing that meditation is about defocusing, I saw that the next step was to simply choose to defocus the mind from the outset. Focusing takes willpower, but defocusing is about relaxation. The secret is to simply relax into the big picture, which creates the effect of calm alertness — the perfect combination for a martial artist. With this insight, I was free of my need for stargazing, because I could relax into the big picture anytime or anywhere — a giant step forward.

At that time I was working in a factory that had a large pond surrounded by a grassy area. Some coworkers of mine were interested in learning martial arts from me during lunch hour, so we went to the pond every day to practice and to eat lunch. After doing so for about a month, I began incorporating meditation into the training. I taught them to sit and gaze across the pond and calm themselves.

There were three young men sit-gazing, so it didn't usually take long before someone began talking, which would rip the rest of us out of meditation. Sometimes we talked about our meditation experience, other times, the martial arts. In either case, we were talking and not meditating.

Although I felt I was heading in the right direction with sit-gazing, I didn't like that conversation was such a big distraction. As a martial artist I didn't like that I had to sit to meditate. A true master, after all, should be calm and alert even in battle. For me, doing anything other than sit-gazing seemed too challenging. The feeling of dissatisfaction returned.

CHAPTER 3

Awareness Games

My dissatisfaction with meditation continued until I got a job in shipping and receiving for a publishing company. I worked in a sprawling warehouse filled with pallets of books more than six feet tall. As I walked the hallways of the warehouse, I realized that I couldn't tell when a person entered or left, or where they were at any given time unless I happened to be in the exact position to see or hear them. As the job was not mentally challenging, and as I always sought to incorporate training into my life in creative ways, I thought I could use the sprawling mazelike aspects of the warehouse to train my awareness.

I devised a game that would challenge my awareness all day long. The basic idea was to expand my awareness throughout the warehouse to detect where other people were. If I noticed someone before they noticed me, then I survived the imaginary assassin's attack. But if someone addressed me before I noticed them or approached me successfully from behind, then I was killed by the assassin. I hoped training in this way would give me the sort of sixth sense martial arts legends are said to have had.

The game kept me attentive throughout my work shift. Over time, it appeared I was making progress, but there was no way to be sure if my sixth sense was really improving, as I was the only scorekeeper. I kept playing the game, all the while wondering how I could verify the quality of my method. Would my heightened awareness be there for me in a time of dire need?

Several months later I got my answer. My company joined a softball league, and I was recruited onto the team. Apart from one player, Mark, the accountant, a former college-league infielder, most of our members were short on athleticism. Mark could throw a softball at astounding speeds. He hit a two-by-six fascia board with one of his throws and split it lengthwise. It was intimidating!

We lost our first few games by many runs, so some teammates decided to bring beer onto the field with them to enhance their enjoyment of losing. After a few more games I joined in, and we all played at various stages of drunk. We lost by greater and greater margins.

One time, deep into a perfectly losing season, in a game with me playing drunken pitcher, a batter from the other team hit one of my pitches into right field. It hit the ground, bounced, and was caught and pitched at first base. It went way over the first baseman's head, to home, where the catcher retrieved it. The runner crossed first and headed for second. The drunken catcher beamed the ball right of second base. It rolled into the outfield. There it was retrieved and tossed to third base and caught. The runner turned around and sprinted for second. Third flung the ball at second, but it went high over the baseman's head, into midfield. Mark ran for the ball. By the time he got it, I was watching the runner cross home base.

"My lord, we suck," I said, laughing as I chugged my beer. Suddenly I felt a piercing pressure drilling into the back of my head, and before I knew what was happening, my body spun around 180 degrees and my left hand caught the ball just in front of my face. The ball was inches from knocking me into the next world.

Mark, the accountant, had beamed the ball at me while I wasn't paying attention. Outside the scope of my conscious awareness, my body must have sensed the threat and taken action. I can't explain it any other way.

We lost that game with a 0-30ish score. It was utterly humiliating. At the end of the game a number of players commented about the miraculous catch, saying in essence that they were sure I was going to get hit in the head. I credited martial arts training for the catch. My palm was achy for several days. If that ball had hit the back of my head ... it's a frightening thought.

Maybe the awareness game had awakened my body, I speculated. I was motivated more than ever to keep working with this active meditation. I loved how it blended well with my daily life.

CHAPTER 4

Motivating Meditation

We're about to get into the nuts and bolts of some very powerful meditations, but before we do, I feel it important to warn of the potential dangers that can come from heightening awareness. As with almost everything worth doing in life, there are potential dangers.

Sometimes the path of unfoldment can open us to some extraordinary phenomena that we might not have previously experienced or thought possible. As the conscious walls that have been boxing in our awareness begin to dissolve, we may experience "psychic phenomena" or what could be called miracles. We might have a premonition that is vivid and perfectly accurate. We might experience a powerful healing, encounter "spirits," or have profound visions from which we gain valuable insight.

These things surely sound wonderful, and who would not wish for these experiences? But as with anything in life, attitudes and motivations are vital to the experience. Although there is no guarantee that extraordinary things will happen to everyone walking the path of unfoldment, they happen often enough that I feel it merits discussion of the potential dangers. Because I was once pulled off the path thanks to impure motivations, please allow me to share the experience in hopes that you will not have to go through a similar painful experience.

When I was growing up I had a number of visions of the future. Some of these visions occurred while I was asleep and others while I was awake. As I became an adult, I began spending a lot of time in deep meditation and prayer. Sometimes these deep sessions would bring me to indescribable states of love. Sometimes, amid these prayer-meditations, I had out-of-body experiences and premonitions of the near future that were perfectly accurate. These strange experiences began occurring with enough regularity that I began wondering if I were psychic.

Upon considering this possibility, I remembered my mother having a premonition that saved her life when I was young. She came shaken into the house one afternoon. She told us of an experience that she'd had just moments earlier. My family owned a horse ranch, and my mother boarded and trained saddlebreds. She told us about a particularly ill-behaved horse that she had just been riding. She said she'd always had a funny feeling about this horse, but she had dismissed it until the night before, when she had a bad dream about the animal. She said the dream was just so realistic. It had color and depth that was far beyond a normal dream. In the dream she rode the horse down our driveway, which has a sheer 15-foot drop-off along one side. At some point on the ride, the horse spooked for no apparent reason and started shuffling sideways toward the edge of the bank. The horse went over the edge, taking my mother with it — and my mother awoke. The next day, when it was time to ride that horse, she got on its back and said to herself, "It was just a dream, so quit worrying and start riding." She rode the horse down the driveway as usual, and at exactly the same place, the horse spooked and began side-shuffling toward the cliff, just like in the dream. My mother couldn't dismount on the left side because that would send her over the cliff, and she couldn't get off on the right because she had a weak ankle that she feared would break. She remembered, in the dream, that she and the horse went over sideways, which could be fatal, so, with no other option, she turned the horse toward the cliff, hoping that the horse would see it and stop before going over. Instead of stopping, as would a normal horse, it just went over and slid down on its hooves. Miraculously the horse stayed on its feet, and my mother stayed on its back. Thanks to the warning of the dream, they both emerged unharmed. The animal was later diagnosed as being mentally impaired.

What struck me most about the whole situation was just how clearly my mother was shown what was going to happen. It was as if the dream was a warning. I wondered if there was some sort of psychic gene that was passed through her to me. I needed answers, so I determined to search for someone who could help to clarify my experiences.

I met a self-proclaimed psychic, Jorge, who was reputed to be "spot-on accurate." Jorge was extremely effective at "reading" people. At first I thought it was a trick, but then he "read" me. The first thing he told me was that I studied martial arts. I thought, he probably learned this fact from the acquaintance who introduced us. Then he told me that although I studied arts stemming from a number of Asian countries, I was most focused on Japanese martial arts, especially those of the samurai. I had not told my friend these things, so my interest was piqued.

He went on to tell me that I had a learning disorder, "dyslexia" as he called it, and was colorblind, something he could not have known by any earthly means that I knew of. He told me details of my learning disorder as well as my character traits. He spent about an hour with me, telling me a large variety of things, precisely — not like the vague readings that are hallmarks of most "psychics." Considering the many visions that I had as a child and my recent metaphysical experiences, I had to accept the possibility that Jorge's readings were authentic.

Unexpectedly, Jorge asked me to be his teammate on his teaching tour. He wanted me to be his bodyguard, chauffeur, and martial arts teacher in exchange for his teaching me about psychic phenomena and how to communicate with spirits. He explained that he did not actually read people, that instead it was a spirit he spoke with which was reading people. I was excited at the prospect of finally understanding what I was experiencing, and even more excited at the thought that I might be able to use these abilities to help people.

I lived and traveled with Jorge on a teaching tour through Mexico. He was trying to break through "the Catholic hold on the communities" in order to get people interested in "real spirituality," as he described it. He taught about the spirit worlds, predicted the future, gave readings, gave speeches, participated in debates, and led marches. It angered a lot of people. Jorge was concerned about the possibility of violence, so I participated in all events as a protector.

Jorge was extraordinarily confident, charismatic, and affable. Throw in the ability to read people precisely and you have a perilous combination. I lived with Jorge in Mexico for six months, which gave me a chance to see a tremendous transformation. When I first met Jorge, I was so impressed by his humility. He described himself as merely being a vessel through which "spirit spoke." He said, "Any power or wisdom that you see is not mine, but of the spirit that is with me. I am just like a puppet. Don't forget that!" But as Jorge became more popular, received rave reviews, and developed a following, I noticed that he began believing that he was the one who was special. And the more that he indicated himself as having the power, the more inaccurate his readings became.

Before long Jorge began claiming privately that he

was the savior of the world. It seemed to me that the "spirit" that spoke through him was no longer running the show — if there ever had been such a spirit. Things were getting culty too. People were following Jorge's advice without consideration, which Jorge encouraged. If someone did not follow his advice, he spoke of them in front of others as being "off the path."

I was getting quite concerned over Jorge's rapidly deteriorating behavior and the obvious inaccuracies of his readings. I also started noticing that there was a certain tension among the women in the group. Because I was always with Jorge, as an apprentice, a teacher, and a bodyguard, I was regarded highly; thus, many individuals came to me to discuss their troubles. By this means, I discovered that Jorge was sleeping with many of the women, most of whom were married. The husbands were not yet aware, but it would not be long until they figured it out, I thought.

I confronted Jorge with my observations. He tried to quell my concerns with money. He had a very wealthy donor, who had given him a nice car. He assured me that if I stuck by him, we would be living the high life. He bragged about how much money he was making from his wealthy followers. I left.

I wondered how I had been so duped. On the

surface it appeared that Jorge was the only one at fault, but I knew that I had played a part in being fooled. It occurred to me, in a flash of insight, where I had gone astray. I had been prioritizing psychic phenomena over truth, over love. Time and again I had felt a transcendent love, but it was the feeling of power I got from seeing the future that had most captivated my attention. Yes, Jorge spoke of unconditioned love as being primary, but talk is cheap. I was at fault because my motivation was not entirely pure. The desire to know the future can be quite alluring, for uncertainty is what humanity fears most. Fear of uncertainty, and the desire to have special powers, had led me to this cult-in-the-making.

Over the years I have been blessed to see how the desire for certainty seduces many, and how the desire to be special pulls "spiritual leaders" off the path of awakening. All such behavior stems from a profound sense of insecurity that destroys integrity. I am not saying those psychic phenomena are corrupting. It is the motivation that I am indicting. Spiritual awakening is in part awakening from unconscious desires. Realizing that I was susceptible to such hucksterism, I made it a point to watch myself carefully, to watch my motivations, to watch my thoughts, feelings, and words, all good practices for anyone, in any position.

After living with Jorge, I realized that mystical experiences do not necessarily go hand in hand with wisdom, truth, or love, although they certainly can, as happened to me. We must be ever watchful, having no assumptions with regard to mystical experiences and teachers, for there are plenty of both capable of leading us astray. We must take responsibility for our individual paths. Pay attention to what people do, at least as much as to what they say — especially yourself. Go with love, and with service; be careful.

CHAPTER 5

True North

Just a few months after leaving Jorge, I had the Isness inspirience I wrote a little about in the Introduction. Although I have written of the Isness inspirience elsewhere, a lot remains that can be learned from it. What follows is just one example.

My ankle, freshly broken while preparing for a karate tournament, was giving me intense pain. I decided to meditate myself beyond the pain, while simultaneously using the pain to help me maintain attentiveness, something that is difficult to do for long periods.

I used intention and breath with the goal of floating out of my body, and away from the pain, but instead of floating out of my body, I felt that I was getting lighter and lighter within it. With each breath my mind felt a little lighter. Before long I hit what felt like a wall that was blocking my ascension. I searched for any thought or feeling that might be hindering me. I released each blockage that I found with my breath. I had a lot of resentment and forgiving that needed to be addressed. Soon thoughts ceased, but flashes of feelings, disharmonious in nature, still emerged from the unconscious. I acknowledged and released them with my breath and intention, growing even lighter within my body.

After a time my body began to feel transparent, and then, although my consciousness seemed still centered in the body, I felt as if I were traveling the universe *within* my body. First, I encountered the consciousness of Earth, then the solar system as a whole, the galaxy, and then the entire universe. It felt as if I went through spirit worlds and even heaven before I found myself in a great void, and just beyond it was a presence — an intelligence, and love that was all-encompassing. And as soon as my attention went to it, I was immersed within that presence.

I was in the midst of what I assumed religious people would call God. In truth, the inspirience is beyond my capacity to articulate in any way that feels right. To call it an intelligent, loving presence feels palpably inadequate, even though those words are the best I can find. I wish words could describe this inspirience, for if there ever were anything worth talking about, this is it. But the truth is that words trivialize, for words are devised by the mind to cut up experience into understandable, communicable chunks. Because Isness is indivisible, words can never equal the inspirience. Being honest, words can't even equal experience. Although words can describe function, they cannot describe the nature of reality.

Through intention I asked this presence, "What are you?" Its answer, as best as I can describe in words, was, "No other than you. There is no other." This response baffled me because, despite my inability to see myself as being *it*, as an answer it felt perfectly right. This presence felt to be in and throughout all that is, which would, of course, include me, but what I could not understand was how I could be *it*, and yet be unaware of that fact for my entire life until that moment.

The Isness inspirience proved to be both a blessing and a curse. The blessing was in the transcendent nature of the inspirience, for it provides a perspective that one can never forget — that all is one. The curse, in part, lay in my utter inability to articulate the inspirience to people around me. How frustrating it was to have tasted of this mighty elixir yet be unable to pass it around to others in need. The other part of the curse was in the realization that my life was almost entirely out of alignment with Isness. The inspirience was so incomparably profound, so right, that living a life in accord with Isness became my goal. I wondered how I could rectify myself so that the sense of separation would diminish, allowing for constant inspirience. I lacked a process for rectifying myself, and that was painful.

It took me years to figure out that passion was a key factor, and that I would need concrete goals incorporating passion to keep me on the path in daily life.

Passion

As we move ever closer to pure tools of meditation, it is vital that we begin defining goals that will serve to keep us on the path. We need to have an inner compass to orient ourselves, for without direction, we will be sidetracked by the suffering of existence. We need something to keep us oriented toward the place of deepest awareness and unconditioned love within, so that we do not tarry by the roadside when times are tough.

Isness became my abstract compass point, which I moved ever toward through the practice of martial, meditation, and healing arts. My passion for these things gave me purpose and kept me heading in the right direction over time. Of course, I wandered a little to one side of the path or the other, from time to time, but that is normal and natural. Nothing in nature moves in a perfectly straight line. Consider your process to be more like a snake moving generally in the right direction. It goes a little to the right and a little to the left as it meanders in the general direction of unfoldment, little by little experiencing greater aliveness, authenticity, innocence, and authority — ultimately, unconditioned love.

Take some time to clarify your own compass point. Where are you heading? Make your north as defined as possible or you may run out of steam early for lack of purpose. Be sure to consider where you will be in a few years if you continue exactly on the trajectory that you already follow. Would the result of that trajectory satisfy you in a few years? What would happen if the worst parts of you got behind the steering wheel of your life? What would your life be like after a few years of that? If you want to be moving toward alignment with Isness, purpose is your ally. In fact, if you want to do anything of value in life, purpose is key. Surprisingly, a lot of us who are eager for unfoldment lack a clear sense of purpose, and until we find purpose we are, in effect, deeply blocked.

The truth is that when we lack purpose, our lives feel meaningless. Conversely, when we have passionate purpose, our lives feel meaningful. People naturally project their feelings onto the world, so by bearing this thought in mind, it becomes clear that having a purpose gives us a sense of meaning, even if we can't clearly articulate that meaning. With regard to unfoldment, purpose can keep us moving forward on the path, compelling us to face our inner demons, to take on challenges, and to be of service.

Lack of purpose is a terrible form of suffering that consumes you one depressing day and one anxious night at a time. Individuals who tend toward depression are drained of all inspiration, which causes life to appear dull and heavy. Impotence permeates the mind, leaving the individual unable to make even the slightest impact in the world, despite the desire to do so. An individual whose tendency is toward anxiety will become increasingly tense and nervous, unable to relax and enjoy the inherent beauty of all that *is*. In either case the individual is effectively blocked from inspiration.

We all want inspired direction in life, but many of us live lives of obligation and duty, void of inspiration. Nonetheless, some of us have an unconscious feeling of nihilism, which denies that there is any meaning or purpose to human existence or to life in general. Nihilism manifests itself in a mental narrative like this one: "What's the point? Nothing I could ever do means anything in this vast universe. I'm just dust in the wind." This feeling suffocates inspiration and is a real blockage indeed. Many times within such individuals there is a desire to avoid taking any responsibility or making any commitment.

To make progress we must realize that everything is interdependent, and that all action and inaction comes with consequence. The active path of unfoldment is not for those who shirk responsibility. Still, some individuals have been so overwhelmed by their interpretation of life that they feel they can't take any more. For such people, it is vital to pay attention to the inner narrative, which is often a larger part of what is overwhelming them. When the narrative ceases, it is absolutely astounding what a person can go through without ill psychological effect. Counterintuitively, many hardships become sources of empowerment once we realize that we are actually up to these tasks. Regardless of the particulars, all of these issues block inspiration and unfoldment.

Lack of inspiration causes our lives to feel hollow and pointless. This feeling is even more pronounced in individuals who are walking a spiritual path, because they are typically more sensitive than individuals not consciously unfolding. So how do we find our inspiration, our direction, our purpose?

The path of spiritual unfoldment is found in the moment. If we fail to move when inspiration comes, then no matter how much we meditate, no matter how much we pray, no matter how kind and compassionate we appear to be, there will be a feeling of meaninglessness that will permeate our lives and pull us ever deeper into depression, anxiety, and inertness.

If we acknowledge that inspiration comes through consciousness to be shared with the world, then a very simple solution emerges, which is to take some sort of immediate action to birth that inspiration into the world. If we fail to act upon inspiration quickly, it begins to fade in short order. As we turn away from inspiration, the flow dwindles. Once we've made a habit of not acting upon inspiration, it may cease to flow entirely.

So how do we get the flow to start again? Typically people have so filled their lives with duty and obligation that they have allocated no time to do what they are passionate about. Maybe we do not see that our passions are productive, so we discard them as being childish. Reconsider that notion.

One student was so focused on obligation-based productivity that she cut herself off from inspiration.

The effect on her was a strong tendency toward willfulness in daily life and in her unfoldment process. Willfulness runs counter to the unfoldment process, so she was struggling quite a bit. I asked her what she was truly passionate about. She said she loved making pottery, but she had stopped doing it because she could see no profitability in it, and it was just a hobby. In her mind, she did not want to waste time on a trivial hobby. As a result she had almost cut off her source of inspiration. And inspiration is a highway of spiritual unfoldment.

I advised her to take up pottery again with passion, to set aside all thoughts about practicality with regard to her pottery-making time. The next time we spoke she was on fire with passion. Her voice was uplifted, and she said she felt like her spirit was alive again. Her inspiration was bubbling over, and as a result opportunities began to open for her. She met new people thanks to her hobby, and that changed the atmosphere of her life and her mindset. She began observing how she had unconsciously prioritized her life according to the values of society. As a result she began consciously dedicating more time to activities that she was passionate about. Creativity and inspiration became a torrent for her.

We need to distinguish between activities that are spiritually fulfilling versus ones that leave us feeling hollow in the end. I used to play a lot of video games. Simply put, they were fun and exciting. I was good at them, and I liked getting better. During weekends I could spend more than twelve hours playing video games. I did so for years. I noticed that, as fun as the games were, at the end of the day, I often felt a lingering sense of regret or hollowness, as if I had wasted my time. My body seemed to be telling me that there was no meaning in that activity — which is not to say that everyone will feel just like I did, but pay attention to the feeling in the body during and after activities. Make note of the activities that are fulfilling. Spend more time doing those activities. Also, note those activities that result in hollowness or regret. Spend less time doing those things. We can wean ourselves from meaningless activities and gravitate more toward meaningful ones.

Individuals who feel completely uninspired need to take a slightly different approach. First, go and buy a pocket-sized notepad and a small pen. Keep them in your pocket at all times. Whenever any interesting idea comes along, write it down immediately and date it. As I said earlier, inspiration comes through to be acted upon. People who feel no inspiration are people who have a habit of not acting on inspiration when it arrives, so they are inspiration-constipated. To birth inspiration into the world, make sure to write down any feelings and ideas within five minutes of receiving inspiration. This will help to get the flow started again. Thus begins a virtuous cycle that ultimately leads to the realization of a greater purpose for your life, your compass point.

Inspiration is of consciousness, and therefore it is not inherently limited by practicality. Inspiration could be a hobby, or it could be starting a business. It could be writing a book, or raising your children with love and integrity. Really, it could be almost anything. Take a small step back from duty, obligation, and unfulfilling entertainment. Embrace what inspires and watch what happens. You'll feel inspired, and before you know it your spiritual unfoldment process will flow forth at full throttle. Life has meaning, and you are alive!

Now go get that notepad!

PART 2

The Basics of Unconditioned Meditation

CHAPTER 6

Unconditioned Meditation

The Isness inspirience became a template of sorts for my assessment of the various meditations that I explored. As Isness is undifferentiated, its awareness is all-encompassing, which is to say that its awareness does not get trapped in the differentiations and definitions of self, but instead runs right through every separating force, while still being aware of those forces.

To me, global awareness from the deepest place of being became the gold standard of meditation. By practicing global meditation I was moving ever onward toward my goal of daily life inspirience. This gold standard began transforming my meditations, making them more holistic at every level. I knew I had to keep it simple, for complexity tends to fail more often than simplicity when under pressure. There is power in simplicity, so long as it has basis in principles.

I was constantly seeking methods that I could apply in daily life with as little effort as possible. Ultimately, I was interested in transcending meditation entirely, so that inspirience was no longer limited to meditation, but was fully lived. With that aim in mind, I was seeking to understand the principles behind meditation and what it was that pulled me out of meditation. Understanding these elements would allow for rapid unfoldment, I felt.

The more I explored meditation, the more I began to feel that systematized meditations, which require chanting, visualizations, special breathing methods, and so on, were not well suited to daily life applicability. Of course, the various meditations I had practiced had their benefits, so I am very thankful for having explored them, but I felt formal meditation methods were too cumbersome to fit seamlessly into daily life experience, which can be high-paced, stressful, and varied. The greater the alignment with Isness the meditation is, the more it applies to daily life, I felt.

I began working more with the awareness game, feeling it was going in the right direction because I could play it during daily activities, even if only in the background of my mind. As I practiced this game more and more, I realized I was employing sight and sound, but leaving out other senses. I had read that the sense of smell is deeply connected to memory and the unconscious mind in general, so I began incorporating smell into my game. To my surprise I found that smelling allowed for greater relaxation once I became accustomed to it.

After realizing that the sense of smell allows for greater relaxation I decided to include a little awareness of taste as well. I began peripherally paying attention to the sense of taste and the feeling inside the mouth while I played my game. It worked!

There was one sense still missing, however. Around this time I began taking survival lessons. The instructor taught a meditation that focused on feeling the entire body. It was quite a nice feeling, so I included body awareness in the game, along with all of the other senses. It's tempting to think that employing all of the senses globally in this manner would be highly stressful, but surprisingly that is not the case. The trick, I found, is simply not being willful about the process. It takes a bit of practice to find this light approach to global awareness, largely because we have become so habitual about focus and willpower. When things lighten up into global awareness, the game is actually quite relaxing.

I tried it first lying down, and there was a wonderful feeling of spaciousness in the body. I then did it while sitting with no problems. The next test was to determine whether it could be done on the move, and sure enough, with a little practice, I was able to pull it off. At first it took a lot of effort, and I was sure that I must have looked somewhat zombielike. But with continued practice, the zombie effect lightened up. With more practice, I was able to experience that inner spaciousness while moving and appear totally normal.

I tried it at work and found that I could do it very well, but talking caused the spaciousness to collapse, so I began working with talking to see if I could overcome this hurdle. I found I could maintain spaciousness quite well if I just allowed conversation to be in the background of my awareness without hyper-focusing, a strong temptation early on. I also noticed that looking directly into someone's eyes caused collapse, yet not looking into people's eyes might seem rude. Eventually I became able to put a person's eyes in the center of my visual field without actually focusing on them, which allowed for meditation during natural conversation. Clearly, I was onto something with this meditation.

The meditation I was practicing at this point benefitted my daily life, the martial arts, and my survival training, with elements of each area harmoniously incorporated into the meditation method — Isness as the goal.

The Observation Meditation

The observation meditation is an extremely useful tool for unfolding our metaphorical paper, and it is the springboard from which we will discover deeper and more powerful tools of unfoldment. While there are many, many beneficial aspects to this meditation, which I will expound upon later, I would first like the reader to get some experience with the process before getting intellectual on the topic.

I recommend the reader run through the meditation steps in light meditation. Once you have done a rough practice while reading, try it again without reading.

Set a timer to 15 minutes for your first session and add a few minutes each session thereafter if possible, gradually incorporating more and more activity into your daily routine. Regarding position, just make sure that you are relatively comfortable when you sit.

Note: We will be working with the senses here, so in the event that you are missing any of the five primary senses, just do what you can, as the brain will compensate for what is missing. Thus, you will end up at the same place as anyone with all five senses.

Gaze straight ahead, taking in the entirety of the visual field, but do not strain the eyes with effort. Most people will be able to see almost 200 degrees horizontally and about 100 degrees vertically. The highest visual resolution will be at the center of the visual field, where there is full color and detail. Whereas focused vision is highly detailed, peripheral vision is more sensitive to shades and motion at the expense of detail and color. It is the enhanced sensitivity to motion of peripheral vision that helps the eyes detect the faint twinkling of stars. Focusing on a star counterintuitively makes it harder to see unless it is one of the more prominent starts — Polaris, for example.

The peripheral field of vision that you are now

experiencing is what your eyes are constantly feeding the brain. The reason that you aren't typically aware of the entire field is because of selective attention. Your brain automatically cuts out peripheral visual information that does not apply to your current activity. For example, while reading this book, you'll probably be highly aware of a certain portion of the text but visually unaware of the room that you are inside. Awareness of the big picture comes only when we make that awareness a priority. Give yourself a few minutes to acclimate to the total visual field before moving on to the next step.

Once you become familiar and comfortable with the total visual field, begin to include the entire audio field into your awareness by allowing all sound to come into the body without focusing on any particular sound. We can avoid hearing bias by intentionally including all sound without bias. There is no need to be in quiet space for this activity because all sound is acceptable. You could even do this exercise in a noisy room.

Next, become aware of the sense of smell and the feeling of air traveling through the nostrils and into the lungs. You may notice smells in the room, the smell of your own body, and the smell of food eaten earlier in the day. Just allow the various smells without getting caught by them. Do not be concerned in the least if you don't smell anything, as noticing particular smells is not our goal. Instead, open up the senses in an unbiased way without concern for the details. Give yourself a little time to acclimate to unconditioned sight, sound, and smell before moving onto the next step. Relax.

We now move on to the sense of taste and the feeling within the mouth. You will probably be able to taste some or many of the things that you have eaten throughout the day, but in the event that you do not, have no concern. Just relax into the sense of taste and whatever other sensation (warmth, moisture, hardness, softness) the mouth offers. The balance of relaxation and aliveness is vital here. Give yourself a few minutes to acclimate to the sense of taste while remaining unconditionally aware of all other senses.

Finally, become aware of the entire surface area of the body. Pay attention to the feeling of the clothing and air touching your skin, the feeling of gravity pulling on the body, the floor or chair beneath you, and so on. Be careful not to focus on any particular points on or in the body. If you have aches and pains, disallow attention from focusing on those points, and instead grace the entirety of the body with awareness, while still noticing all previous senses. Remain unconditionally aware of all senses in this way for the remainder of your meditation time, with the intent of using less and less focus as you proceed.

At this point, we are seeking a perfect, spherical awareness that extends equally in every direction from the center of the body. The way to tune to sphericality is to start giving some attention to all directions through feeling, but do not be too willful; instead, relax into it. Gradually, we will become more functionally attentive to the total space around us.

You may notice that your feeling tends to stop at walls, ceilings and floors. This result stems entirely from sensory habit. There is no reason that your intention must stop at any fixed point. As you notice your feeling stopping, lightly intend to stretch feeling through and beyond barriers. This is the way of Isness. We are not seeking to feel specific things or to gather details; instead, we are seeking unconditioned intention, unconditioned feeling, unconditioned awareness, and ultimately unconditioned being.

Try to remain in this meditation for the entirety of your allotted time. Once you become comfortable with the process, try it standing and then moving. Add in more difficult activities like fast walking and even running, once you feel up to the challenge. Remember the feeling of spaciousness that you get from this meditation and see if you can maintain it through whatever challenges you take on. Explore your current limits and challenge them little by little, tackling the easier ones first and working your way gradually up to greater and greater challenges.

In the process of your meditation, it may be tempting to add extra elements from previous teachings. I highly recommend not doing so, at least initially. Keep it simple; keep it pure. Allow yourself the time to get the hang of this process and to gain faith in the perfect tools of meditation, found natively within the body.

As I pointed out in the Introduction, there are many scientifically verified physical and mental health benefits that come from meditation. With regular practice, you will find all of these extremely powerful side effects are gained through the observation meditation, but that practice has its greatest results in the realm of unfoldment. Practicing the observation meditation can create a feeling of ever-increasing expansiveness, which helps the meditator to see the self from a nonpersonal perspective. As inner spaciousness increases, little by little one begins to take life less personally, including the self. This nonpersonalizing is tremendously beneficial, as it slowly inoculates us against pettiness, selfishness, and personal attacks, including attacks from the inner critic. It is as if the sense of self has become more transparent, so negativity is more likely to pass by harmlessly. You become less reactive to things not worth reacting to, which, of course, removes a lot of unnecessary but all too common suffering.

There are some other commonly reported benefits to this meditation as well. Many practitioners also report that they are aware when someone is watching them. Suddenly they feel attention on them, so they look, and sure enough, someone is starring at them or following them. A number of individuals also report that their bodies have become "awakened," moving independently to evade unseen dangers, much like what happened with me on the softball field. Although these benefits are fantastic, if we are on the path of unfoldment they are not the main reason that we practice this meditation. All is one; there is no other.

Comfort in Meditation

If we are sitting for any length of time, we may begin to suffer from comfort issues related to our physical positioning, especially if we have chronic lower-back or joint pain. The rule for proper posture during meditation is simple: Be as comfortable as possible without being totally physically slack. There is no need to take a formal meditation pose. Just sit comfortably without being too lax in posture. If we sit stiffly, we will tire quickly and suffer from a lot of soreness during meditation or afterward. Moreover, if we have an overly stiff posture it will create a hyperfocused mind that tires rapidly. The secret to meditation is the balance of comfort and alertness, especially early in the process.

If sitting on the floor, we can use two mechanisms to remain alert through meditation. The first is to keep a slight uprightness of the spine, but without any straining. The spine does not have to be perfectly straight, especially if you have back issues or misalignments. There just has to be a little alertness. For many people, lifting the spine perfectly upright causes pinching of nerves, which our bodies will inform us of eventually, if not immediately. Meditation need not be willful. In fact, the effects are more powerful when we are not being willful.

We can also use our fingertips to remain alert. For example, Buddhists create certain hand poses that fulfill the purpose of alertness, such as putting the tips of the thumbs together while placing one open hand on the other, palms up. The effect is that there is a circle created with the hands. But we do not need specific hand poses to get into a good meditation. It's necessary simply to keep a little aliveness in the fingertips. A basic and highly practical method, for beginners, is to keep the fingertips slightly afloat, not allowing them to rest on anything. If your hands are resting on your legs, for example, make sure that your fingertips hover just above your legs without touching. This keeps you from losing alertness and falling asleep.

If sitting on the floor is not possible, consider sitting on a chair. If sitting is not comfortable, we could lie on our backs. The main danger of lying on the back is falling asleep and/or overarching the lower back, which may begin to smart. For individuals who have lumbar issues, it is generally advised to bend the knees so that the soles of your feet are on the floor and spaced apart at a comfortable distance.

Because we are lying down, we need to have some mechanism to keep us from drifting off. There are two primary mechanisms that we can use to facilitate alertness. If we choose to bend our knees, our job is to keep the bent knees pointed upright, so that they don't start drifting toward one side or the other. The second method is to keep our lightly clenched fists up in the air with our elbows resting on the floor.

For some individuals, lying on the back is just not

possible without experiencing severe pain, so instead of lying back, we could lie on our side. Just choose the side that is more comfortable to lie on. Again, the trick is to create relaxed alertness by keeping some body part afloat. We can facilitate this requirement by putting a palm on a hip while keeping the elbow aimed upward, into the air.

If in the process of keeping our knees, fists, or elbows aloft, they lose circulation, we can lower them until blood fills them again before raising them once more. Just be sure to create a little alertness with the fingertips during such blood refreshing.

Regardless of the position that we choose, we should be mindful of the principle, which is to relax into meditation as much as absolutely possible without losing alertness and falling to sleep.

If you aren't able to remain in any comfortable position for more than a few minutes, then just switch from position to position, while maintaining expansion through the transitions. Because we are seeking to graduate to movement anyway, the pain-necessitated transitions are a perfect opportunity to advance your capacity to meditate while in motion. Continually embrace challenges, for doing so will make you stronger.

Final note: Comfort is relative. What was

uncomfortable for you today could become comfortable in time. For example, I am quite comfortable training in the martial arts, running, or engaging in any number of other seemingly strenuous activities, so meditation supports those activities. Begin testing your comfort zones and expanding them, so that meditation can accompany you throughout your life.

CHAPTER 7

Moving Past Mental Rebellion

While the observation meditation is extraordinarily powerful and surprisingly easy to do, we still may find it a challenge from time to time. The temptation is to give up on such days, but that is the last thing we want to do. Meditate anyway to see if you can transcend the frustration. It happens to everyone from time to time, so you are not in the least alone. I've certainly had my days.

Although I never had a formal meditation teacher, I was fortunate to learn an extremely valuable lesson from an unexpected teacher, who helped me to transcend distraction and mental rebellion during meditation and throughout daily life. I'd like to share this lesson with you in hopes that it helps you to get more out of your meditation and life.

My wife and I regularly visited a large park in Tokyo for weekend strolls, for picnics, and to walk the dogs. One day at the park a young Japanese girl unwittingly became my teacher. We had agreed to meet a friend, Yuuji, for a picnic one Sunday. Yuuji brought his wife and his eight-year-old daughter, Kotomi, and we brought our dogs.

One of our dogs, Leila, is a small Chinese crested dog, as members of the breed tend to be. Kotomi really loved dogs and wanted to walk one of ours, so we let her take the lead for Leila. Kotomi was so excited to walk a dog for the first time! It would also be Leila's first walk with a stranger. My wife taught Kotomi how to hold the leash, how to keep Leila next to her during the walk, and so on. Kotomi listened and nodded that she understood.

Our little Leila was always great on walks, but as my wife handed Kotomi the leash, Leila looked at me incredulously. Clearly this encounter was going to be a battle of wills. Leila totally ignored Kotomi's lead and began sniffing here and there to her heart's content.

Kotomi, feeling Leila's weight on the leash, pulled the leash over her shoulder and leaned into the walk, forgetting all technique.

Not wanting to submit to this stranger, Leila leaned back against the leash and bucked against the girl. Kotomi just kept moving forward as if Leila wasn't even there.

I kind of felt bad for Leila, but she wasn't experiencing any physical harm. She was testing her new walker, which is not uncommon for dogs that have never been walked by anyone other than their family members. Curiosity had me, and I wanted to see how this scenario would play out.

Leila put up a great fight, but it was all for naught because Kotomi seemed oblivious to it. She was just excited to be at the park. I wondered if she had forgotten that there was a dog on the other end of the leash. The dog fought; Kotomi just moved forward.

After five minutes, I began to wonder how long Leila could keep up her fight. Ten minutes passed with Leila still locked in resistance mode, so I considered taking the leash myself. But then, like the flipping of a light switch, Leila joined the walk.

Just like that, she surrendered to Kotomi and seemed to smile as she walked next to her new friend. For the rest of the day she was the perfect dog. She sniffed, wagged her tail, and even let Kotomi pick her up, the first stranger ever to do so successfully. Kotomi had won a fight that she never even took part in! She just moved forward mindlessly.

After this experience I began applying the "forward motion" principle to my meditations to astounding effect. I just gave up any expectation that my mind was going to cooperate and instead simply moved forward.

How does that principle play out in meditation?

You know how it can be in meditation: the mind gets distracted again and again. The mind may be caught up in some physical aches and pains. Then the mental resistance starts with statements like, "I'm not doing this right," or "I have too much mental noise," or "I don't feel like meditating today; I'll do it tomorrow instead."

But now is the only time that we ever have! Tomorrow never was and never will be. It's a figment of the imagination. Either we are moving forward in the moment or we are not.

Admitting the reality of now, I decided to sit in meditation for the allotted time, regardless of how my mind felt about it. I was not going to let distraction or

64

frustration have any power. I determined to let the mind fight the good fight, while I moved toward my goal of deeper relaxation and clarity.

My mind was worried about work-related issues, reminding me of things that I already knew. Here's what happened.

"Did you check the tests for grammar errors?" I took a deep breath, tensed my entire body and released it, relaxing my body and expanding my awareness globally.

"Don't forget to print the tests first thing tomorrow morning!" I tension-released again, going deeper still into relaxation, opening awareness again in every direction.

"Remember to ...." In midsentence I tension-released into spaciousness.

I noticed that my mind would go into little frustrated narrations as a thought arose: "Jeez, another thought," or "Ah, again," or "When is this going to stop?" Then it occurred to me that my reactive opinions of thoughts are also thoughts, so I decided to relax and expand at each such occurrence.

After a few minutes of expansive releasing, secondary thought ceased, but there was still the feeling of frustration when primary thoughts arose. I then included feelings into my breath-releases.

In short order, thought felt far away. Although thought still occurred, there was no feeling that it was *my* thought.

The breath-release-expansion continued at each distant thought, and after a time overt thought and emotion ceased entirely. What was left were just little blips of thought and emotion, unformed and out of context. They came up, out of the unconscious like little ripples in the stream of awareness.

I had a sudden insight into how the mind worked. Thought begins with these tiny little blips that the mind reacts to habitually by stringing them together with memories, effectively creating narratives, stories, and images that pull awareness out of the present.

This realization was like seeing behind the curtain in *The Wizard of Oz*, only to find a weak-willed con man at the controls. A debilitating illusion was broken.

Silence ....

The lesson of moving forward worked. Just like

every little step that Kotomi had taken in the park, so I moved forward, step by step, into a timeless clarity that was interrupted only by a beeping alarm. Thirty refreshing minutes had passed.

So, when you sit down to meditate, decide how long you are going to be there and be there for that allotted time, relaxing ever deeper into expansiveness. Accept that the mind will sniff here and there and rebel. Just keep moving forward through relaxed awareness into spaciousness.

Eventually something unexpected may happen. Before long the mind begins to follow your intent, silencing quickly.

When you stop fighting the mind, something else unexpected may happen. You may also cease to concern yourself over the mind's assumptions, opinions, narrations, regrets, instant replays, and so forth.

Once there is insight into the mind through direct experience, there is no longer any need to fight or correct it. The dog will come along once it tires of the fight, and before you know it, you will have a new friend who supports your meditations — and your life.

CHAPTER 8

Appreciation

After the Isness inspirience, all I wanted was to live a life in accord with Isness. I ached to return to that consciousness, but no matter how I tried to reenact the meditation that got me there, I was utterly blocked. I felt it was my sense of self and the inner disharmony that was revealed during the inspirience which was preventing me from returning to Isness. I didn't know how to resolve the inner disharmony that was giving rise to my sense of separation. Frustration gradually built up over time. Finally I prayed for an answer, which I received several years later in an elevator dream.

I boarded a crowded elevator and pressed the button for the top floor. As the elevator neared the top, it suddenly jolted to a halt. We opened the door to find that we were stuck between floors. Everyone was nervous, not knowing what to do. There was a snap and the elevator dropped down a few feet. Another snap and the elevator was in free fall, the digital floor display rapidly counting down to our deaths. People were screaming in blind panic, realizing that there was no escape. Knowing that these were the last moments of my life, I wanted them to be my best. I allowed my life to flash before me. I felt a great appreciation well up within as I opened my arms to welcome the final moment. "Thank you," I prayed as I extended my total appreciation to life, the good and the bad, for I had learned from all of it. In that moment, there was not an ounce of fear. I was totally free and ready for departure. Suddenly the elevator began to slow and it smoothly touched down on the ground floor.

I awoke from the dream in that moment, knowing this was the answer to my prayer. The secret to living inspirience is total appreciation for all that is. My job was two-fold. First, I was to embrace the present moment as completely and passionately as I could. Second, I was to clean up everything within me that was blocking appreciation.

Finally, I had a clear direction to follow. I did my very best to employ unconditioned appreciation, to see where I fell short. It didn't take long before I realized there was a lot of time during the day when I was not in appreciation. But at least I had direction and some idea of the steps I would need to take to begin the resolution.

I had no tools for resolving my blockages, and several years passed before I had a vision that hinted at the tools I would discover to resolve those blockages. I saw that by combining the martial and healing arts I was studying in Japan, a new art would be born that would at once serve to protect, to free up inner blockages, to heal, and to enlighten. I told this vision to my martial arts instructor, and to my surprise, he was intrigued. He suggested that we exchange knowledge. I would teach him therapy, and he would teach me martial arts. We met together privately and explored these arts for hours each day to see what came of the collaboration.

After some time, we discovered a certain feeling in the body that came as a result of the therapy. If we applied our intent to that feeling, then we could use it to greatly enhance our martial arts performance. We began playing with global meditation to determine whether we could create the feeling in our bodies purely through intent in meditation. It didn't take long until we were able to repeatedly find the feeling. The closest word I can find that describes the feeling is a totally vibrant, open, unconditioned appreciation. Maybe it was what the dream and the vision were guiding me toward, I thought.

I began applying this feeling to my life. Each morning, first thing, I took a few minutes to tune to unconditioned appreciation. I repeated this meditation on the train to work, on breaks at school, during lunch hour, in the dojo, on the train ride home, while bathing, and finally before going to bed. I tuned to appreciation in any spare moment. My martial arts skill soared, inspiration became a torrent, and my life, in general, was lighter, brighter, and more full of meaning.

Appreciation Meditation

Using the same global awareness principle from the observation meditation, we can reach the next plateau through the feeling of appreciation. First get yourself into a good observation meditation. Once you are firmly rooted in global awareness, think of something for which you have a pure feeling of appreciation.

71

Once you have that thing in mind locate the feeling of appreciation in your body. Many people will feel appreciation in their chest. The more appreciation we feel for this thing, whatever it may be, the more powerful will be the effect. A truly deep appreciation will have a palpably powerful effect.

Now that we feel appreciation, let go the image and pay attention only to the feeling in the body. See if you can feel appreciation in all parts of the body simultaneously. You may notice that you can feel appreciation in some areas more than in others. It is possible to feel it everywhere evenly, but we may have to practice for some time before that occurs. Allow yourself to acclimate to the glorious feeling of appreciation in the body.

Now begin sharing the feeling of appreciation globally, just as you did in the observation meditation, but try not to be overly willful about this. Enjoy it, even as you relax into global appreciation. Look at the objects around you and feel the appreciation flowing through them. Remain in the place of unconditioned appreciation for as long as you can, but pay attention to what it is that takes you out of this meditation, for that is where you need to work, so that it no longer pulls you out of appreciation.

Each time you practice this meditation, see if you

can find a word that automatically fills the entire body evenly with deep, vibrant appreciation. If we find the right word, the body will feel like it's vibrating with energy. Truly it's an amazing experience that can then become a guide for our next process.

With true inspirence, everything will be unconditionally vibrant with appreciation, for you will see how everything can be learned from, even the horrors of the world. This result may seem to be an impossibly high bar, but it is the way of Isness, which ultimately means it is your way. Despite the perceived difficulty, it is better to work toward appreciation than to give up. Make a little progress every day, and just keep moving forward, while being especially attentive to feelings of resentment. What you will find is that your capacity for appreciation will grow over time. Things that you could not accept before gradually become more digestible as appreciation shines through you more and more. Change what you can; accept what you can't change — until you can. Appreciate all of life. That is the way.

CHAPTER 9

Reprogramming on the Fly

Let's get a little scientific here. If you're interested in meditation, chances are that you've heard the term *neuroplasticity*, a hot word in the meditation community. It is also referred to as *brain plasticity* or *neural plasticity*.

Until fairly recently, neurologists believed that the brain changed very little once an individual reached adulthood, but recently, thanks to improvements in technology which have allowed us to observe changes occurring in the brain, we now know that the brain changes throughout our lives.

Neuroplasticity has been observed from the microlevel of individual neurons to the macrolevel of cortical remapping. The important takeaway here is that the brain is constantly remaking itself on some level, and we can take advantage of this fact. Whatever you pay attention to or practice during your waking hours gets reinforced in the brain when you sleep. During sleep, resources are removed from pathways that are not being used and allocated to pathways that had been stimulated during the day. Realizing how the brain changes, we can begin to consciously stimulate what we wish to reinforce in the brain. If you are not practicing global appreciation daily, then you will not be making much progress. Even a few minutes every day helps. Use it or lose it, as the old saying goes.

So, how do we make use of neuroplasticity with regard to unfoldment? Simple: Your brain is habituated to react in certain disharmonious ways, ways that are counter to unfoldment, ways that create folds. Realizing that we have counterproductive emotional and perspective-related habits, we can begin to make changes via the principle of neuroplasticity. Here's how I began retraining my brain.

When I first started training martial arts in Japan, I

was surprised that my instructor allocated only a few seconds to meditation at the beginning and end of each class. How can one meditate in such a short period of time, I wondered? I found it perplexing, but considering that my instructor was recognized as a top-level martial arts master, I was certain that he must have had a good reason for his methodology. After all, there are few people on the planet who have more expertise in the martial arts than he does.

I asked my instructor what I should do during meditation, and he said, "Just empty your mind." It sounded so simple, but I wondered why it was just for a few seconds. He said it was my duty to figure that out for myself. That is how these arts are passed down; students have to discover the secrets themselves, with the instructor serving as the ideal to aim for. I pondered this matter for quite some time before the answer came to me.

I realized that samurai had to put themselves into a heightened state of clarity within a flash, for any method that was long and drawn out would be insufficient for instant action. Although I had no way to be sure, I began playing with flash meditations throughout my days working as a junior high school teacher.

Junior high is an extremely challenging work

environment because most of the kids are going through puberty almost simultaneously. One day a student is like an angel, and the next the same individual can seem like a demon. Even if you ask them why they are misbehaving, in many cases they just don't know. What can you do with that? Needless to say, frustrations can run high.

I made a game of flash meditation. Because I knew that I had to look at the clock regularly throughout my lessons to get through the steps of my lesson-plans in the allotted time, it seemed a good idea to use the clock as a reminder to flash meditate. Inspired by the elevator dream, I was interested in incorporating appreciation into my life, so I started flash meditating to generate the feeling of global appreciation during my busy day.

Here's how it worked. Whenever I looked at the clock, I would take a mental picture of my inner space. It was usually quite noisy in there because of the nature of the work, so I meditated the feeling of calm appreciation. I would only give it a few seconds of attention.

I found it quite challenging at first, but after a few weeks, I was consistently able to reach a clear, spacious appreciation and remain in that feeling for some time before it faded into noise. Once I realized that flash meditation worked, I began applying it as soon as I noticed my inner space getting small and constrictive. As soon as my mind narrowed in negativity, I flashed into appreciation. After practicing this approach for several more weeks, it became rather effective.

I was unwittingly taking advantage of neuroplasticity, and so should you. The degree of importance that you allocate to the practice determines the degree to which the brain responds, but don't get too willful. Take this activity seriously and make it a priority in your life, and it will prevent a lot of future folds, as reactive patterns fade. Doing so will take time, but it is sure to be time very well spent.

PART 3

Unbinding Conscience

CHAPTER 10

The Conscience

After the Isness inspirience, I realized that almost everything that we've ever done has been to some degree out of alignment with Isness, which creates disharmony. No wonder we do not live inspirience. At some point in the unfoldment process the individual chooses to embrace an integrity that transcends opinion, belief, religion, culture, language, and everything that we've ever been taught.

Realizing that our perception of reality is largely bound by the conditioned structures of belief, culture, religion, language, and so forth, and that those very same structures have created the disharmony which is veiling Isness, the individual begins deeply questioning those structures, feeling into their nature within the body, for resolution can begin only amid awareness and feeling. After thorough exploration, one discovers a great deal of disharmony is bound in conscience. Simply, much of what we have or haven't done has weighed us down. There may be much fear, regret, shame, blame, guilt, resentment, anger, and pain — all born of a sense of separation.

The Nature of Conscience

There are two primary forms of conscience: learned, and that of Isness. First let's explore the nature of learned conscience. By exploring learned conscience through feeling and awareness, another, deeper conscience may be revealed.

It is a biological imperative that children play, which is to say a child's psychological well-being actually depends in part on play. Children need to play and are strongly motivated to do so. Thus, it is in their best interest to interact with other children in a way that grants opportunities for sustainable play. For such opportunities, the child must play fairly. Of course, young children don't necessarily recognize that fair play equals continued social access, so it is the job of parents to teach the child about fair play. A child who does not play fairly will soon be shunned by other children.

Many children at age three are extremely selfish, and it is only because of their drive to play that they can be enticed to modify their behavior. Play is the carrot that lures them into being a little less selfish than they would otherwise be at age three. If a child does something antisocial, such as lie or cheat, the parents, hopefully, will tell the child that their action wasn't fair — that the action was wrong. After repeated corrections, the parent's voice becomes incorporated into the child's "conscience." Of course, as the child ages, the voices of other people — teachers, pastors, coaches, employers — add to learned conscience to create an individual who can function well in society. As the individual matures into adulthood, being seen as contributing to and supporting the culture and society in which the individual lives becomes increasingly important. We apply the label *cultural conscience* to this broader extension of learned conscience.

Cultural conscience is about fitting into society, not about fairness. Thus, cultural conscience can create some odd effects out of the context in which it was learned. For example, many foreigners feel really uncomfortable when they go to a Japanese noodle shop and hear people slurping noodles — which is how soba is supposed to be eaten in Japan. When foreigners learn that they're supposed to slurp, cultural conscience may warn strongly. There may be a pronounced feeling of disgust at the experience. Is this function of conscience useful? It would be in our home country, certainly, because slurping noodles would be considered a rude or sloppy way to eat. You might have trouble getting a date if you eat that way.

For individuals who are highly open-minded, cultural conscience may be easy to set aside when abroad, so for them I include a grosser example that is sure to trigger almost anyone's cultural conscience. We can take advantage of the triggering by noticing where, in your body, disgust is felt. My apologies.

Consider booger eating. All children, even primates, do it naturally up to a certain age. Primates never stop, but people do. Why? Is it because eating boogers is bad for you? No. Eating boogers is actually very good for you because various pathogens get caught in the nose's mucous, which dries. When crispies are eaten, the body's immune system is triggered and adapts to those pathogens. Booger eating is an instinctive, scientifically verified, natural form of vaccination. If society didn't teach children not to eat boogers, we'd all be eating them — and be healthier for it. That feeling of disgust that you feel right now has been programmed into you, yet it is not beneficial to you biologically. The feeling has nothing to do with fairness. It is purely a social construct.

Where did your cultural conscience show up in the body when imagining booger eating? Can you articulate the feeling? When you see a person eating a slimy one, what are the thoughts running through your mind? Make note of them. The narrative goes something like "Ew! Booger eating is disgusting," and "He's so disgusting," right? The booger-eater is actually doing something good for the body, according to science. Knowing this, is he still labeled as disgusting?

You will find "booger conscience" remarkably powerful because you fear how others will judge you, and you assume that boogers taste nasty. Very few people want to be labeled as disgusting, and having gone as long as you have without eating one, you're not about to start now, are you? That said, if you are going to partake, might I suggest that you do it in private? No, your car doesn't count.

Cultural conscience can be reprogrammed, which usually occurs to some degree when people move abroad. A cultural conscience that doesn't fit the new society in which we live is not helpful at all. To be comfortable in a Japanese noodle shop, unless you are very "open-minded," you have to reprogram cultural conscience not to warn against slurping noodles. I went through this reprogramming while living in Japan. I found the experience quite enlightening. Boogers ... thankfully for me, Japanese people shared my disgust.

We can see that cultural conscience can be reprogrammed, as is evidenced by people who move abroad and choose to embrace a new culture, but what about moral conscience? Can we reprogram our conscience with regard to lying, cheating, stealing, or murdering? Surprisingly, we can.

Cultures that have roots in English common law share the idea that everyone is, at a fundamental level, valuable — even a criminal. In such cultures, innocence is assumed and guilt must be proven. If we were to immigrate to a country where common-law human rights are not enshrined, however, such as Saudi Arabia, and we were to embrace the values of that country, then our conscience would change to represent the newly embraced value-system. You might find yourself lining up with the crowd to watch criminals being dismembered or beheaded. Most people living abroad pick and choose what they adopt from the new culture, whereas some may never assimilate, remaining outsiders, but reprogramming is certainly possible if you wish it or have a highly mutable personality.

The realization that learned conscience is fluid can be terrifying, for we may believe that without our learned conscience, which comes from our family, culture, and belief-systems, we would remain in a selfishly chaotic state like that of many two-year-old children. If we assume that learned conscience is the only thing keeping us from becoming sociopaths, then, yes, we are heading quickly in a very dark direction, for selfish desires would go entirely unchallenged. In fact, there is a strong argument that removing someone from a particular value-system or religion without replacing that system with some other value structure is highly damaging to the psyche. The individual will be suddenly lost in a sea of unmitigated desire. The statement "God is dead" from Friedrich Nietzsche in the late 1800s rocked the world. People wondered what would keep them in line without a Heaven to entice and a Hell to deter. Moreover, without a God to give them meaning, people lamented the purposeless suffering of life. Nietzsche's idea proved to be a blow to the human psyche from which we have yet to recover.

The modern sense that life is meaningless was uncommon before Nietzsche's proclamation. Without religion to delineate morality, to lend meaning to human lives, morality and meaning came to be seen as subjective. Initially people flocked to science as a replacement for religion, but science necessarily sidesteps morality. Lacking any moral compass, science and its byproducts inventions can *and will* destroy humanity, given sufficient time. Morality and ethics reside in human beings, and those qualities must guide science, not the other way around.

Fortunately there is a long overlooked alternative for what has been lost since the decline of religion. This replacement is a human birthright, one that, once revealed, cannot be usurped. I call it innate conscience. Since the evolution of self-consciousness, innate conscience has been waiting for revelation. Innate conscience is not rooted in the mind-children of religion, philosophy, science, or idealism; instead, it is born of a sense of connection to all that *is,* often inspirienced during states of deep meditation. Quite naturally when one inspiriences *oneness with all that is* the desire to take advantage of others vanishes. From a connected consciousness, to steal from someone else is to steal from yourself. Thus, to the degree that one lives inspirience, integrity shines forth into the world. Although innate conscience is our birthright, few have realized it. The time has come for innate conscience to shine forth — beginning with you.

At first, innate conscience is quite subtle, but with repeated inspirience it becomes ever more tangible. To discover innate conscience, we must first clearly understand the nature of learned conscience, which is to say, we must be able to clearly feel it in our bodies. Although we have experienced learned conscience countless times in our lives, until now the experiences may have been largely reactive, which is to say unconscious. To consciously experience learned conscience we must explore the feeling of it in the body. Through the exploration of feeling in the body, we may also begin unveiling innate conscience.

The exploratory process is quite straightforward. Simply remember back to the last time learned conscience spoke clearly to you. You might remember a time when you stole something or lied in a very big way. While remembering, notice where in the body you feel conscience. For most people, the feeling will be in the abdomen or diaphragm area, but the location may vary a bit from person to person. Once you feel the location of "your" conscience, allow a little time to acclimate to the feeling in the body. Is it a positive feeling or a negative feeling? What adjectives would you use to describe the feeling in the body? Give yourself a few minutes to explore conscience before reading on.

It's not a pleasant feeling, is it? That's because learned conscience is born of shame, blame, guilt, frustration, anger, fear — all the negativity that your parents, society, and you were feeling when the voice of conscience was instilled and reinforced within. Learned conscience is dark.

Now, let's discover where cultural conscience resides. Simply remember a time when you willingly partook in some sort of social faux pas. For many people cultural conscience speaks from a higher location, like the upper chest or even the head. Do not be concerned if yours is located elsewhere. All that matters is where cultural conscience resides in your body. How does it feel in the body? Are there any adjectives that describe it? Give yourself a few minutes to explore cultural conscience.

Cultural conscience isn't pleasant, either. How could it be otherwise? Its root, after all, is the notion of otherness. Although learned conscience is unpleasant, it is a vital phase in human development that ultimately leads us to innate conscience. Innate conscience is quite pleasant, for it comes of a sense of connection to all that is. While innate conscience can't be defined, we can say that awareness of it begins by consciously feeling into the body, just as we did with learned conscience.

For now, let's say innate conscience resides in the awareness of inner space and the sense of connectedness. In terms of function, it is fair to say that innate conscience detects when inner space is distorting or shrinking in any way. The more natural the sense of spaciousness, the more precise is innate conscience. As I said earlier, defining Isness is virtually impossible, as to define is to limit. The same is true of innate conscience, so for now please accept that my description is merely a functional place to begin. Much like Isness, innate conscience is not to be defined, for to do so is to feed the sense of separation. Being attentive to inner space and connectedness takes you in the right direction.

CHAPTER 11

Diminishment

According to ancient Egyptian mythology, when an individual dies he or she is judged in the Hall of Maat. The process is simple: only an individual whose heart is as light as a feather may enter into the heavenly kingdom of Osiris. Weighing your heart against a feather is an absurd concept if we take it literally, but if taken metaphorically, it is extremely useful for unfolding souls. The "heart," your inner feeling, truly does get lighter through the unfoldment process, leading to a heavenly inspirience in the moment. There is no need to die to enter Heaven. In truth, the Hall of Maat is within you. There is no way to escape, for it is the Heaven and Hell within that judge. What is rooted in Heaven (oneness) inspiriences Heaven. What is rooted in Hell experiences Hell (separation). This Truth applies to every moment of your life.

As we ignore conscience, there is a distortion, a negative atmosphere within. Studies have shown that children begin distorting reality to gain advantage as early as age three. The more intelligent the child, the earlier they are likely to play with distortion for selfish gain. Impatient children who lack the ability to compete tend to gravitate toward distortion as a means of getting by. Instead of working to develop socially acceptable competitiveness, they may resort to cheating and lying. Often such children lack mentors to help them correct inappropriate attitudes.

How do we define a lie? If you were to ask ten people, you might discover that the answer varies somewhat from person to person. As unfolding souls, we need precise definitions to make progress. Lying, cheating, and so forth are actions of deceit, so deceit is where we will focus our attention for now. The *Merriam-Webster Dictionary* defines deceit as being *the quality of being dishonest or misleading.*

For the purposes of unfoldment we will say that deceit is any action or inaction, which includes thoughts and feelings born of the sense of otherness. For unfolding individuals, this definition of deceit will become increasingly more useful as we go. For the time being, take note of any action or inaction, thought, or feeling that disturbs inner space. During such disturbance, the body is actually physically weaker for a moment. The more we pay attention to the causes of inner disharmony, the greater is our awareness of what is blocking us.

Deceit

I once had a chance to speak with a former inmate who served time for stealing. Theft had been his full-time occupation. I asked him to recall his first experience with theft. He told the following story:

I first stole from a kid that I didn't like. He was a bully, and I wanted to get back at him somehow. So I decided that I would take something from him. I got the idea from some friends of mine who were into stealing. I was uncomfortable with the idea at first, but the more I thought about how he bullied me, the more I convinced myself that he had it coming. I talked myself into it — that it was the right thing to do — to teach him a lesson. It took several hours before I was ready to do it. I pumped myself up with anger. I used anger to justify a lot of what I knew to be wrong.

After that, I started stealing more and more, but at first it was only from people that I didn't like. With each success, theft became easier, requiring less justification. Eventually, I stole from anyone, even my own family. I became the leader of my group because I was the most ballsy. I would do stuff others were afraid to do, so they looked up to me, which I liked.

In retrospect, it was so stupid. It's all downhill once you turn off your conscience. I got into drugs. Then I sold drugs. I know people who died from drug overdose. Most of my old friends served time in prison, became homeless junkies, or died. I knew what I was doing was wrong, but I would never admit it — stealing was so easy.

This individual put his finger right on the origins of deceit. Deceit has its roots in the desire to do what is expedient above all else. For him, stealing was the easiest way to fit in, as his friends were into stealing. They were children who did not learn to play fairly, who lacked patience. Maybe their parents failed to instill conscience in them between the ages of two and four, the vital age window for socialization. This individual was surely rejected by well-socialized children, which explains why he was hanging out with youngsters who were into stealing.

Thought enables deceit, even if the words do not immediately precede the overt expression of deceit. For example, if an adult were to behave in a cowardly manner, a thought like, "I'm a coward" need not occur in that moment, although often it does. Cowardliness was probably embraced long ago, usually in childhood with the thought identification, "I'm a coward." Self-denigrating thoughts are completely out of accord with Isness. They create a negative atmosphere, which later expresses in the world. Thoughts have the power to enslave the individual!

If we were socialized sufficiently by age four, we probably don't live antisocial, criminal lives, but we all play with deceit to some degree.

"I'm going to start working out" — weeks later we're staying in.

"I'm going to start saving money" — the bank account keeps shrinking.

"I'm going to cut down on sweets" — days later we're molesting the cookie jar.

Seemingly "harmless" self-deception creates a lesser feeling of diminishment than does stealing, like a grain of sand relative to a boulder. But because self-deception is so easy, it quickly turns into a vast sand dune, weighing us down from within. Every time we make false statements, whenever our words do not match reality, there is inner distortion, a diminishment, a fold. With each diminishment, we are even less able to follow through, our self-respect shackled. And with each unexecuted goal, a little more clarity is lost, causing more stress, anxiety, depression, aimlessness, and feelings of futility.

There is a point when people become so diminished that they stop making any goals whatsoever. They quit trying to do anything challenging or meaningful. This diminished state is extraordinarily depressing and agonizing, for it is usually accompanied by chronic pain. To regain our inner space and our spiritual authority, our thoughts and words must resonate with integrity.

In cases of extreme diminishment, it is vital to set very small, doable goals. Then, as they are accomplished little by little, the sense of empowerment grows within. In this way, we can work our way up, gradually, to greater and greater challenges. As with anything, a lot of small steps tend to take us further than the big ones, which can destabilize our centers and sap our energy. Persistence is the secret.

Once we realize the price we pay for not keeping our word, we can begin making productive changes. Until then, we are simply doing what is easiest in the moment unconsciously.

Each time thought or expression is out of alignment with Isness, there is a diminishment, something you can clearly feel if you pay attention to the body. When we say something that we are not truly behind, there is a feeling of distortion, disintegration, and weakness in the body. With active lying there is obvious inner distortion, disintegration, or collapse of energy. When we make flippant goals, our energy tends to rise into the head, leaving the rest of the body feeling flat. Oppositely, when the goal is in harmonious accord, there is a feeling of integrated wholeness. Simply do less of what causes weakness and more of what supports wholeness. This process is one of correction — you will make errors. It can't be helped. Just keep moving forward, one baby step at a time. The accuracy of innate conscience will improve gradually as what blocks awareness thins.

The body doesn't lie, so let's honor it as our teacher. The more we listen to the body, the quicker the unfoldment. And each time that we listen, sensitivity to inner space becomes ever clearer, making it still easier to detect when we are going astray. This way the self becomes the transparent vessel from which Isness shines forth. There are countless ways in which deceit has bound our souls. I will guide us through a few of the forms that deceit can take. As I run through some of the various areas of deceit, pay attention to learned conscience as well as innate conscience to enhance your awareness of the differences between them, and to heighten sensitivity to the inner space — a hallmark of the unfolding soul.

The Inner Critic and Boastfulness

"I'm heartless," "I'm not good enough," "I'm a failure," and so on are but a few of the seemingly endless array of possible self-denigrations. Anytime the inner narrative tries to diminish you, and you believe it, it has succeeded. Although it may be true that mistakes were made, certain skills need to improve, and some behaviors should be corrected, it is utterly useless to personalize the critique. Isness never personalizes anything.

To stop feeding self-denigration, take account of your most common denigrating narratives. What is your inner critic telling you? Once you have a narrative in mind, replay the last time it sounded and pay attention to the inner body. Where does that voice reside?

Many teachers recommend that we talk back to the narrative, attempting to counter it with positive statements. For example, we may follow, "I am cowardly" with the counterstatement "I am brave." Such advice is for individuals still playing in the dream of self, not for unfolding souls. "I am" followed by anything diminishing or inflating is a lie, for Isness transcends words.

Feel into the narratives, the positive and the negative, and you will see that they are based in comparisons — that is, otherness. If the inner narrative says you are strong, to whom is the comparison being made? Someone weaker, of course. Isness never personalizes, compares, or identifies with anything in particular, for to do so would cause collapse. Isness is your true nature, and when thoughts are not in accord with that nature, inner space becomes small and distorted. Isness doesn't require compliments, and neither do you.

Following the principle of nonidentification, pay attention to the moments when the inner narrative inflates the self. In that moment there is an inflation of the inner body that feels strong to the unaware. Although there is an inflation of energy, there is also an imbalance, which causes tension. This condition is strong compared to the diminishment that comes of self-denigration, but this strength is nothing compared to the power of the transparent self, something that you will discover in time if you remain diligent on the path.

Why? Isness sees all things and does not compare them. The mind makes such comparisons for personal gain. Whenever the mind tries to inflate self-image, it is simultaneously putting down others. After all, if you are strong, to whom are you comparing yourself? Someone else must be less strong than you to make that comparison. The unconscious mind is constantly responding to your word choices. Words and feelings that are not in alignment with Isness cause the imbalancing effect. Seeing the nature of the inner narrative lets us stop feeding it through belief or through counterstatements.

One of my martial arts students once boasted, "I'm getting good at this technique." I admonished him not to be so careless with the mind. I asked, "To whom are you comparing yourself?" He said, "Compared to other students." "What makes you think that any of them are good at this technique?" I asked.

"... Ah ...."

I said, "I would never say that I am good at this technique because I know there is a lot of room to improve. And to whom would I be comparing myself? To those who aren't as skillful. Since I'm constantly seeking to improve, comparing my skills to those who are less skillful doesn't help in the least. Be ever mindful that there is no set limit to how good one can get at any given skill. A careless statement like 'I am good' is false from the outset. 'Good' is only relative to people that are less 'good' — a useless comparison. Make your goal continual improvement. If you said that you were improving, I would agree with you. But do not think that you are good. It's poison. As Lao-Tzu says, 'Be careful as a warrior in enemy territory.' The enemy territory is your own mind. There is no other."

Idealizing

What about when we mentally inflate others with such thoughts as "She is perfect," or "He's so cool"? Pay attention to your inner body when thinking these things. To whom are you comparing these idealized people? Certainly, idealizing has diminished at least one person in the process — you. As the old saying goes, if you think someone is perfect, it is just because you don't know them very well.

Observe others without condemnation or praise, for looking through the eyes of the other is you. If you look in your heart of hearts, you may recognize that the thing that you most want is to be truly seen. What greater compliment could there be than to really see, to really listen to others, as if you shared the same soul?

As you begin to "see" people, idealization begins to fade, for fundamentally, all is one. Almost everything that we have been taught in society is contrary to our true nature — Isness. It's no wonder that so few individuals ever inspirience Isness.

Flattery

With most of us there is a spirit of insecurity lurking just under the surface, hoping for a good compliment — "You're so cool," or "You're so beautiful," or "You're really good at that thing you do," — but by now you can feel that there is something not quite right about such statements. Many times the people saying these things are just unaware of the implied comparison and admission of not truly seeing you. After all, compliments are largely rewarded in modern societies.

That said, it is very important to show people that you do actually see and care for them. As a teacher, I will let people know when they are heading in the right direction in their training with a statement like, "That's getting much better," or "You're heading in the right direction," but I will never compliment generally with a statement such as "You are good at X," because it is false. If I want someone to know that they are better than I am at a certain thing and I think I could learn from them, I will just say as much. Precision with our words is very important.

So, there is the well-meaning compliment, but there is also manipulation. Children catch on to complimentary manipulation quickly. "Mom, you're the best," or "Mom, you're so beautiful." A wise mother asks, "What do you want?" because she knows the kids are buttering her up to get something. This form of manipulation continues into adulthood with many people. Be ever watchful of people who are highly complimentary, for those compliments are not free. Often such people are seeking to take advantage of you, or they are compensating for a lack of virtue, which is going to affect you eventually. Through compliments, they are attempting to get you on their side. Be watchful of such people, but be just as watchful of your own motivations and inner space. This is the way of Isness.

Snoopiness

The verb *snoop* is defined by the *Merriam-Webster Dictionary* as *look or pry especially in a sneaking or meddlesome manner*. We all know people who do not appreciate our boundaries and who pry and pry to get any morsel of information that isn't relevant to them.

It is a normal survival instinct to fear the unknown, for there is potential danger in unchartered territory — the predators in the darkness. Looking into the unknown is essential for personal growth, wisdom, and virtue, for it is in the darkness that you face your fears and restore inner space.

The compulsion to snoop has nothing to do with personal growth, wisdom, or virtue. Snoopiness relegates the personal lives of others to entertainment. Most of us are not overtly snoopy because we know it will cost us friendships, but in private, when no one is looking, the snoop may lurk. Ever notice how magazines like *The National Enquirer* may catch your eye while you are standing in the grocery line, even if you don't buy them? You surreptitiously read the cover to see which celebrity is getting divorced. When surfing the Internet, do you find yourself clicking on celebrity gossip stories?

Being honest, snooping is a vacuously seductive form of entertainment. Start noticing what happens to the inner space when the snoop has emerged. Where in the body does it reside? Snoopiness is a prison. Awareness is the key.

Gossip

Whereas snoopiness is your personal consumption of other people's private lives, gossip is the broadcasting of that private information to third parties. Begin noticing whenever you speak of others, and be very careful with words. Many gossips will justify that what they are saying is true, so it's okay, but if you simply feel into the gossip's atmosphere, the motivation will become obvious. In most cases, malicious selfishness is rife. Sometimes gossips are just getting high on the attention they receive, and they are not consciously meaning to be malicious, but they can't seem to stop. These individuals are actually addicted to the emotional high they receive from gossiping.

Although it may be fair to warn of a certain individual's tendencies, so as to be helpful, seeking attention by denigrating people is not. Pay close attention to any distortion of your inner body when speaking of others, and be sure to question your motivations.

The inner gossip completely undermines the trust of people around us, for deep down, they all suspect someday they will be the target of your words. Gossip at its best attracts people who will pull you down, something an unfolding soul carefully avoids.

Condemnation

Most of us would seem to be experts at condemnation if mere quantity determined our suitability. But for some reason, no matter how clearly we see others, those people never seem to change as a result of our scorn.

We look at murderers and condemn them, assuming that we would be different were we in their shoes. This assumption stems from the belief that our soul is separate from theirs. We assume we would be different were we born in their body, under the exact same circumstances. We assume we would get it right where they get it wrong. The assumption is both unfounded and arrogant, even though it seems totally rational.

Consider the forces behind every single decision that you have ever made. With each, you "chose" according to the forces of the moment as you felt those forces. You sided with the forces that felt most powerful to you. For example, if you selfishly stole something, there was the force of desire, the fear of getting caught, and the force of conscience to name but a few primary components. The force of desire was stronger than the combined forces of fear and conscience, which is why you stole. It could not be any other way, for you will always side with the strongest force or combination of forces. The illusion is that you can look back on a decision with new-found wisdom, an additional force, and remake the decision. But reality is now, and decisions come from the forces at play now. If you could replay a past decision, you would make the very same decision 100% of the time because the forces at play in that instant are unchanged. Likewise, if you were born in a "criminal's" body and grew up in the same circumstances as did they, you would do exactly as they did. There is no other.

When the self is transparent and the soul is seen beyond the lens of separation, it can be likened to a liquid that is poured into a vessel, the body. The soul conforms to the qualities and flaws of the vessel from which it perceives the world. At a deep level, the murderer is you experiencing through a different set of filters.

This is not to say that you should not be aware of murderers, for that would be naïve and dangerous. Isness is fully and deeply aware of the distortions that lead to an act of murder, discordant thought, feeling or action, and therefore it is right to be aware of such things. Spiritual unfoldment embraces a holistic awareness, not foolish naïvety.

Condemnation is different from pure awareness, because condemnation is based on the sense of separation, feelings of superiority, fear, and / or disgust. There are times when we need to take decisive action regarding a murderer, but such action will be informed by the realization that the murderer is you looking out different eyes. You are also the victim, the family of that victim, and each and every other individual in society. Such awareness is a powerful force that influences your decision as to what to do about the murderer. We really are the world.

When your spouse or children are behaving in ways that you don't appreciate, consider that it is your soul looking out of their eyes. Then consider what would be best for you were they you. When you hate someone, you hate your own soul. When you love someone, you love your own soul. Your soul is everywhere. Love or hate — which do you choose?

Feel into condemnation and the assumptions that support it to see how reflexive condemnation is in your life. Only by doing so can you ever discover how much better your life can be.

Minimization

When someone apologizes for a transgression, it is extremely tempting to minimize the transgression with untrue words like, "It's okay," or "No problem," or "That's fine, it didn't really bother me anyway," even though it did bother you. Minimization comes from awkwardness at the sight of another's pain, and maybe the desire to appear kind. A true apology is uncomfortable because the individual is exposing a weakness and submitting themselves to potential condemnation.

Be honest and tell them how you truly feel without condemnation. You might say something like, "I really appreciate your sincere apology. What you did really put me out. Why did you do it?" If they are authentically trying to reconcile, you might agree to maintain the relationship, or not — it's up to you.

Even though an apology is sincere, do not minimize

the transgression, for to do so is to steal the full lesson of the experience from the individual. Let the person fully digest the apology and the reconciliation without minimizing or condemning. Just be honest, and, if the apology is authentic, you can accept it appreciatively. That doesn't mean that you have to be their best friend again. It's up to you. Feel the inner space for what is right. Don't hesitate to spend time away from the individual for clarity if need be.

Complaint

Although there is an appropriate time for complaint, the vast majority of complaints take the form of sympathy-seeking or frustration-venting, with no intention to correct a discordant issue. Generally, such complaint is indicative of self-identified feelings of victimization and weakness. To hold such feelings is extraordinarily diminishing, and to act upon them by giving them voice in the world is even worse.

If you have a legitimate grievance and intend to correct the issue for the betterment of all involved, it is probably a service to issue complaint, but such complaint will not carry with it a whiny vibration. It will come from a place of principle, a place from which the grievance is more likely to be taken seriously.

Be very attentive to the inner narration and to inner space before issuing a complaint, for those elements will tell you the degree to which the complaint is coming from integrity — after all, there can be a mix of principle and whininess. If there is a feeling of whininess or desire for personal gain from the complaint, it may be wise to holster it for a while until you have more clarity. In this way, we can maintain integrity and forward momentum along our path of unfoldment.

Many situations exist wherein you do not have the authority to make immediate, constructive, external changes. That fact does not prevent you from making constructive inner changes. Pay attention to inner space, where wisdom is waiting to be discovered.

Positionality

A common way for people to inflate their self-image is to teach when inappropriate. We all know those people who show off at every opportunity. The same thing can be said for people in authority who lord it over us. They revel in their advantageous position and use it to inflate self-image. Many times these individuals are quite capable, knowledgeable, or skilled, but they go the extra mile with their position. They may not always intend to be malicious, but the atmosphere that they create is nonetheless disharmonious.

Here's the uncomfortable part. Most of us participate in positionality in some way. We may be inclined to force our authority or to shy away from taking authority when there is legitimate need. Love serves need, not want. When it is appropriate, we teach. When we are short on information, we listen, which usually means we listen even when teaching. But if the motivation is self-aggrandizement, then to teach is to diminish the inner space and bind the soul even further.

Positionality is easily detectable in the body, and paying attention to that feeling when it arises in small matters will make it obvious in large matters. Lead when leading is required, and follow when following is needed. Teach when it is appropriate. Listen and learn when that is right. As the proverb goes, there is a season for everything under Heaven. Conscience will sort the season.

White Lie, Brute Truth

Is it possible to live your life without white lies? You know: those little lies that serve as social grease. I remember once, on a train in Japan, when an elderly woman addressed me. She wanted to practice her English. She introduced herself, and we began conversing. It wasn't long before she began seeking compliments. "Americans look so much older than Japanese people of the same age, don't you think? People are always telling me how young I appear, even for a Japanese woman. How old do you think I am?"

Had I an ounce of common sense at the time, I

would have told her I don't answer such questions, but wisdom eluded me, and I answered, "Seventy." Her face immediately flushed red. "How rude," she said as she turned and walked away. I told the truth, knowing that it was not what she was hoping for. When I recall the situation, I can feel the contempt I had for her compliment fishing. My answer was unwittingly born of contempt — a brute truth.

When someone asks you if their dress makes them look fat, it is tempting to tell a white lie and say, "Not at all. You look great!" — even if you feel otherwise. Rather than lying, it would be better to direct the individual's attention back to their own feelings. Often people aren't as aware of their feelings as you would assume they are. If you watch yourself carefully, you'll realize that you aren't nearly as aware as you think you are, either. Knowing this, we can help people to become more aware of their inner world. When someone asks me if their dress makes them look fat, I might simply ask, "How do you feel in that dress?" Often, asking a person how they feel is enough. If they are still asking for an opinion, I might suggest that they choose a dress that they feel more comfortable wearing. Sometimes people want to feel a little wild. If they pay attention to their feelings, they can find a balance between comfort and sass. Personally, I don't give my opinion on things that people can decide for themselves — that, and I have zero fashion sense.

With regard to brute truths, we all know people

who frankly say whatever they think, regardless of how it makes others feel. If you call them on their rough tendency, they will probably justify themselves proudly as "just being honest." But if you feel into it, they are often saying harsh things intentionally to make others feel uncomfortable. In many cases, brute truths are a form of bullying. Sometimes, brute truths emerge from insensitivity or foolishness, not malice. Pay attention to the feeling within the body to clarify the motivation, while looking out for the well-being of all involved.

Sometimes frankness is required. In cases of drug addiction, for example, a bluntly honest intervention by family and friends may be necessary for the addicted individual to see the harm that they are causing themselves and everyone around them. Be honest through love. If the intervention is rejected, the forces involved in that individual's life may be just too powerful to overcome at the time. Addiction and the forces underlying it can be extremely powerful. Just do your best.

There are situations where the good of everyone may seem to be out of alignment with speaking the truth. Imagine that you lived in Nazi Germany when the SS came to your door to ask the whereabouts of a certain friend of yours, who was actually in your house at that moment. Do you tell the truth and point out your friend, or do you lie? If you tell the truth, your friend may be arrested. If you lie, the soldiers may just move on, none the wiser.

Looking out for the well-being of all souls involved may mean telling a lie. Imagine the Nazi scenario vividly and feel your inner space. Try it once while lying and then again while telling the truth. What are your results? This scenario actually happened to a certain priest, who answered truthfully, "I don't know where he is," for in that exact moment he could not see his friend, so technically speaking he didn't precisely know where he was. Maybe there is a magic answer like that for every situation. I don't know, for I have never been in a similar circumstance. Practice feeling the inner space with small issues and gradually work your way up to ones that are more consequential. Practicing this way will prepare you for the hard times to come, allowing for the best possible resolution to arise spontaneously.

Be honest, but do so in appreciation whenever you can. The unfoldment process will go much smoother for you that way. Honest people will love the atmosphere around you so much that they accept your quirky virtue because they know you are looking out for their best good. Those who can't accept honest, clear appreciation are probably not going to stick around, for they have allied themselves with inequity. What sort of person do you want to attract?

Rationalization

There are so many ways in which rationalization manifests in our lives, but one of the most common ways is with regard to desire. Most of us can remember a time when we wanted something that we knew we probably shouldn't have at that moment. Maybe we don't have enough savings, and purchasing the item would require taking a loan or extending our credit. In any case, we really aren't ready to have the item, but the desire is so strong that we unconsciously begin embellishing the virtues of that coveted thing, while glossing over or minimizing the negatives.

Once rationalization begins, desire is almost certain to be fulfilled because desire has successfully denatured the "rational mind," which now serves to justify desire instead of clarifying the situation so we can make the healthiest possible decision in the moment. One hallmark of highly unfolded individuals is that they have very few desires, and what desires they have are rarely powerful enough to enslave rationality.

As our metaphorical paper unfolds sufficiently, it becomes clear that overwhelming desires are merely patches that hide unresolved inner disharmony. Realizing this principle, we can feel into that disharmony to begin the healing process. When you notice rationalization rising up within, start getting curious about it. Where does it reside in the body?

114

Curiosity is the first step toward transcending desire and rationalization.

Neglect

For most of us, neglect is nearly omnipresent in our lives. We may neglect our health by not exercising, not playing, lacking purpose, not eating properly, not getting sufficient sleep, not having sufficient intimacy. We can neglect our families through work, play, or being scattered or disengaged when physically together. Not providing structure and discipline for ourselves and our families is also neglectful. Structure and discipline are vital nutrients, as are calm, affection, and play.

There are numerous areas in which we can be neglectful, and most of us could probably make a fairly long list of the things we have neglected, if we wanted to do it. Each instance of neglect diminishes our inner spaciousness. Simply walk through your house and see what is calling out to you. How many of those things have been pressing on you for days, weeks, months, or years? Start taking care of these things with appreciation, and begin finding some balance in your life, which probably means, at least in part, greatly simplifying your life.

I find that I am able to concentrate on any one task for only so long before needing to take a break. If I am managing time well, I take a break as inspiration begins to wane, which is typically just before mental exhaustion sets in. During my "break" I take care of things I've neglected. I may organize my desk a little, for example. I allow intuition to determine what I do during breaks. Not being too willful allows for good time management — a balance of productivity, creativity, and organization. If you have reached exhaustion, rest is the only option that doesn't lead to physical and or mental detriment.

If you have difficulty following through on your to-do's, start clearing out the backlog to open up your inner space. Do something small right now. Set this book down, and take care of it. You'll feel so much better for it. The book will await your return.

Tardiness

Tardiness is extremely disruptive to our inner space and to society. Consider the effects of habitual tardiness. First, people who claim to be "okay" with your habitual tardiness are lying to appear generous, have nothing better to do with their time, or are willing to postpone other parts of their lives to accommodate tardiness — not good, in any case. Productive individuals will often stop associating with you once they realize you do not respect their time. That leaves you in the company of unproductive people when you most need to be around capable, productive individuals who support your unfoldment.

A certain percentage of people may maintain relations with you because you have some other redeeming characteristics, but still feel frustrated with you every time you're late. Your tardiness will always be the elephant in the living room. The feeling of frustration is not healthy and will tarnish relationships with these individuals, even if you don't realize it.

Some productive individuals, unaware that you are habitually late, may call around to apologize, postpone, or cancel other appointments to make things fit with you. Your tardiness disrupts countless other people, and you might not realize it because many people won't complain, not wanting to appear petty.

The result is a terrible mess, and we've only touched the surface. Yet another ill effect that ripples through society is the haste that inevitably follows tardiness. You realize at the last minute that it's time to leave, but you have yet to begin preparing for departure. Suddenly you are rushed to do in 10 minutes what should rightly take 20. Nothing goes well under such hasty conditions. You mind is in a whirl as your frustration goes through the roof. You get into your car and find yourself speeding everywhere, cursing under your breath at red lights and "incompetent" drivers in your path. Your heart becomes the size of a peanut, and this is before you are even technically late. As your tardiness has affected others, they are probably suffering from some complementary frustration. And when frustration is high, accidents are more likely to happen. Who knows how much pain and suffering tardiness has caused in your life?

Then there is the awkwardness when you walk into a room with someone whom you feel may be upset at you. Do you give some excuse, a lie? Or do you "play it cool," saying nothing, in hopes that the other person doesn't care? Maybe you have normalized tardiness and don't care what others feel, justifying the behavior with thoughts like "This is just how I roll, and people need to accept me as I am." All of these options are tremendously disharmonious. Even if you apologize, the apology isn't authentic, for you are merely trying to save face. It's arguably better than not apologizing, but it's extremely diminishing.

Cascades of postponements, cancelations, haste, frustration, accidents, and awkward apologies ripple through society because of habitual tardiness. It's hell on the body, but don't take my word for it; feel into it — the body doesn't lie.

Spite

Spite is a form of petty ill will or hatred, born of resentment, that usually shows up during arguments with loved ones. It is a tit-for-tat verbal aggression intended to cause the other person equal or greater emotional pain than we are suffering in the moment. Spiteful words need not be truthful to pack a wallop. All that is necessary is that the target of the words has some insecurity in relation to them. Usually, spiteful words twist or embellish a grain of truth. Even if the spiteful words are factually true, they are energetically false because of the malice behind them.

Spite is considered normal in relationships, even among most adults. Social normalization of spite is what lends it so much destructive power in the world. Spite ruins relationships and inner space. When spite is normalized in a relationship, healthy, productive communication decays, as mirroring between individuals rapidly decreases.

Mirroring is the degree to which people pay attention to each other during interactions. When mirroring is high, the individuals involved function well as a team and care deeply for each other's well-being, with maintenance of the relationship taking precedence over individual desires. When mirroring is low, resentment and frustration cause interactions between said individuals to be antagonistic. Instead of looking for the best in our partner, we are spying for everything that is wrong — which is to say, we are energetically summoning what is wrong. If mirroring gets low enough, individuals give up and detach — intimacy is lost.

Once aware of innate conscience, we begin having insight into the destructive nature of spite and other forms of malice, as we can feel how it collapses inner space. Through direct insight we can see the destructiveness of spite on others, society, and the world. With insight into malice, the individual no longer projects spite, preferring to employ the truth with the best interest of the relationship at heart. This shift does not mean there won't be anger or frustration from time to time, but it will not cross the line into malice. Eventually, malicious intent will cease to arise in the mind, ending spite and so many other forms of disharmony.

Being able to speak the truth is vital to our health, our relationships, and society. Once we believe we can no longer safely speak productive truth, it means mirroring is weak in the relationship. It is possible to salvage such a relationship, but great patience, care, and honesty for the sake of all involved must be at the fore.

Looking at present society, mirroring is at an all-time low, whereas spite is rife. There is a deep chill on the truth, with factional polarization moving ever toward the extremes. Society is near the breaking point. The usual desire is to fix society through policy, but the true solution is brought forth from within us to shine through our personal relationships. Pay attention to inner space and let it be the guide. Nobody wins when spite is running the show.

CHAPTER 12

Refining Conscience

Through the exploration of inequity, we discover that it manifests in many areas of our daily lives. Although I have mentioned a number of areas to explore, much is left to discover in your personal process of unfoldment. If you pay attention to inner spaciousness, I am confident that you will discover the rest for yourself.

You may have noted, as I went through the various forms of deceit, that some areas were more obvious to you than others. For now, we could say that there are multiple volume controls, some of which are turned up higher than others. This difference is a result of learned conscience. As innate conscience comes to the fore, there will be less and less discrepancy between the different forms of inequity. There is simply awareness of spaciousness and that which diminishes.

Innate conscience, born of Isness, is in the cells and nervous system of the body, for Isness is omnipresent. When you are in tune with Isness, your body will notify you instantly. There will be a powerful sense of alignment, integration, and balanced spaciousness. Your body will feel alive, grounded and inspired when things are in alignment with Isness. The feeling will not be excitement, which sometimes arises as inspirience wanes. In such a case, excitement is an unconscious form of resistance. Feel into the body during times of excitement to note its energetic instability.

Alignment with Isness is vital to unfoldment, and this is one of the key areas in which people are largely missing the mark. Most of us like to think of ourselves as having integrity, but the reality is that if we sincerely observe inner space, we will start to notice the smallness. There are some people who dutifully take care of all or many of the noted areas of inequity, but who still suffer from suffocating inner spaces. It's not just what we do that matters, but also the manner of execution. Appreciation through awareness of inner space is the how.

Without appreciation, no matter what we do, the result will be stagnation or shrinkage. The more we practice global appreciation the more sensitive we become to our inner space. Global meditation gives us something to shoot for in daily life, and something to compare our habitual patterns with. Ultimately, we want our daily life experience to be as clear and spacious as are our meditations. When that happens, our lives flow with inspirience.

There are several powerful ways to awaken innate conscience. One of them is appreciating the feeling of innate conscience. If you successfully felt into your inner space, innate conscience has been, at least somewhat, unveiled, and you will hereafter be a little more aware of areas to which you had previously been blind.

Although appreciating the sensation of innate conscience as an exercise is powerful in itself, the best results come through daily life application. Regularly feel into inner space and note what causes expansion or diminishment, for such catalysts are your guides. Do more of what causes spherical expansion and less of what causes shrinkage and distortion.

When your body alerts you to inner disharmony,

you can simply stop, apologize (if need be), and change directions. If you've lied, you could say, "Sorry, my mouth got ahead of me," and then tell the truth. It will be extremely difficult at first to do so, but if you do it once successfully, it will get a lot easier the next time around. If you find yourself making false goals, denigrating yourself, and so on, you could simply cut off the narrative midsentence and correct it by flashing into calm, global appreciation and then continuing forward with clarity.

We may be alerted to inequity on the fly, but often we are so unconscious in the moment that we miss it, and only later do we recognize that something was amiss. Then we can reflect on the day to discover when there was disharmony and take appropriate corrective measures through appreciation. With inspirience, there will be greater and greater awareness and capacity to make corrections on the fly. Daily application is essential to reaching this stage of awareness.

One final note on learned conscience versus innate conscience – learned conscience has a negative feeling and an inner voice through which it speaks, whereas innate conscience feels positive and has no voice. If your inner voice says things like "You are a horrible person because you told a lie," please be aware that

that voice is not of innate conscience, but is, in fact, self-denigration, something that innate conscience warns of once we are sufficiently aware of the inner space.

Enhancing Innate Conscience

Note: The greater the awareness of inner space, the more you will get out of conscience meditation. Also, as you practice conscience meditation, be sure to tend with appreciation to whatever inequities you can.

Warning: This meditation, if done sincerely, will initiate a process that roots out corruption in all aspects of your life. Ultimately, the reckoning is unavoidable, so I advise embracing what may come and using it to perceive conscience. It may not be pleasant, but unfoldment isn't all sunshine and rainbows. Are you ready?

Conscience Meditation Method:
1. Set a timer for as long as you wish to dedicate to this meditation. I recommend allocating at least 20 minutes to get a basic sense of the process.
2. Pay attention to the size of inner space. Is it just a little space in the torso? Does the entire torso feel

open? Does the entire body feel open? Does the spaciousness extend clearly past the body? How far? The greater the spaciousness, the greater the grace. The smaller the spaciousness, the more separate, defensive, and walled off we feel in our lives.

3. Once you notice the spaciousness, simply expand the feeling globally to the entire universe. There is no need to focus on the senses or appreciation for this meditation. Simply pay attention to and share spaciousness with the universe.

4. Now look around you and see what is calling out to you, and take care of it.

Practice this meditation at every available opportunity and watch the situations you find yourself in. Your conscience will be well exercised in short order. If you are sincere, you will be facing a lot of hard choices. Were you expecting any less?

As you abide by innate conscience your awareness of inner space will deepen, providing connectivity, balance, inspiration, insight, and so much more. Give it a year of sincere attentiveness, and you'll look back in utter astonishment at the change.

CHAPTER 13

Putting Feeling to Work

As you can see, conscience is a huge area to work with. If you look at ancient religions, many seem to address the issue of conscience to some degree, but only in relation to form (commandments), not principle (inner space). This shortcoming has left humanity with a dangerous imbalance of intelligence to wisdom. We are clever enough to devise technology that can wipe humanity from the face of the planet. We are not wise enough to realize that, given sufficient time, our technology *will* wipe us from the planet. It is my hope that through the awareness of inner space, the imbalance of intelligence to wisdom will soon be corrected.

I also know how utterly overwhelming it can be to realize the extent of our inequity. Surely there are many things that have been calling out to you, things that you have been meaning to get to, but never do. Maybe you've been meaning to mow the lawn, but the mower is broken. You've put off having it fixed for almost a year, and your yard is a jungle. Your garage is an utter catastrophe, and your bedroom is a mess. Maybe you've been meaning to write a letter to a certain friend for months, but you never get around to it. Or you know that you need to have a talk with that person that you've been avoiding because it's uncomfortable. What of the unattended family issues, not to mention all of the false inner talk, the narratives, and myriad other facets of conscience that need attending to? Where to begin?

The best way to start this journey is with one little step — take care of one neglect right now. Tomorrow, take care of another one. In this way, you can start addressing the backlog of neglect that is weighing on you, diminishing your inner space. I can hear you thinking, "But I just don't have the time or energy. Had I the time or energy, I wouldn't have this backlog of neglect." But the reality is, you have less time and energy precisely because of all that neglected stuff. You feel unclear, and therefore you think less clearly. You have less energy because your house is a drain on you. Everywhere you go, there is something calling out to you to be done. We need to get some momentum going. Take care of just one thing per day, if you can't do any more, but at least do something. Instead of doing the entire garage, try organizing just one thing whenever you go in there. If you are like most people, you probably own more things than can be healthy. You could get rid of something every day.

The benefit that you get from lightening the load depends on several factors. First, of course, is the degree to which you take action. The second relates to the degree of accuracy in which you have taken action. And third, the degree to which you have enjoyed the process. Grumbling your way through the corrective process won't help much, because grumbling causes shrinkage, and because you'll probably give up before long thanks to negative associations with the corrective process. Bearing this likelihood in mind, we need a way to take care of the backlog that will further our unfoldment and bring inspiration to our lives. The meditation below will help get you working on that backlog, get it done precisely, *and* make it exhilarating at the same time! You're going to enjoy taking care of stuff. It's a hard sell, I know, but do it sincerely and you'll be amazed.

Reordering Through Meditation

This meditation activity is one that I regularly teach at my seminars. Every single student who actually did it as described has found it to be exhilarating and productive. I hope you do as well.

Here's how it works. First choose a place in your home to tidy up, a place that has been calling out to you for some time. It doesn't have to be a big job. It could just be a desktop or a corner, something small enough that you can actually do it now. Feel into inner space and expand that space universally. Now tune that space to unconditioned appreciation. Let the intensity of appreciation grow until you notice that everything around you feels brighter. Now allow your body to lead you. Just release the reins and allow your body to go where it feels drawn. If the body doesn't move on its own at first, just follow the inner feeling, but pay attention to the body in the process. What is drawing the eyes? Go there.

Let's imagine that your eyes are drawn to a cluttered nightstand. Notice all of the items there. Generate a deep feeling of appreciation for everything

130

there, as if everything were alive and were about to show you how it wished to be arranged. Now relax and let your eyes be drawn to what needs to be moved first.

Trust your body to move the item to where it *feels* right. We are looking for a feeling of inspiration and integration in the body. At first you may need to move the item around before you find that feeling. The more you inspirience the feeling, the easier it will be to notice next time. The more precise you make the placement of the item, the deeper the feeling of inspiration and rightness will be. Allow yourself to explore this process — get out of your head.

After practicing this method sufficiently, many people report that the body begins to move of its own accord, dusting here, moving an item there, adjusting positions, throwing certain things out, or setting them aside to give away. And when it really kicks in the movements are fast and precise — no thinking involved, just awe. It's an extraordinarily liberating feeling.

Practice this meditation a little every day. Use it to take care of the things that you have been neglecting. Pay your bills this way. Use it to take out the garbage. There are just so many ways that this meditation process can be applied. So you see, there is a way of being that takes care of things and leads the unfoldment process simultaneously. It's a gift that's always been there, just waiting to be picked up and put to use.

Once you start taking care of the nagging backlog, you will find that life takes on a much smoother flow. The appreciation meditation when put in service will be a lot like an Isness inspirience in that you will walk around your house and everything will be communicating a desire for a flowing order. It will be a real pleasure sorting it all out through deep loving appreciation.

It's important to remember the difference between what we are doing, which is rooted in conscious appreciation, and obsessive compulsive disorders associated with orderliness. OCD has roots in deep anxiety and brain chemistry, not appreciation. If we are doing the appreciation meditation properly, there will be no negativity in this process. Make note of any feelings of disgust that may arise in this process. If we are rooted deeply enough in appreciation, even if we find a dead rat under our bed, there will be no disgust.

CHAPTER 14

Pruning the Tree

So, you've begun tending to areas of neglect, and you are beginning to feel clearer inside. It's like taking a nice breath of cool, crisp morning air. But you look around and realize that the work you have done is like pulling a few cans out of a mountain of garbage, and you grumble to yourself, "This is impossible ...."

Think of the Buddha, Jesus Christ, or Lao-Tzu. They have so many commonalities. One obvious commonality is that they all lived simple lives with few possessions. One might assume they abandoned material things out of some religious ideology. But I suspect ideology had nothing to do with their lives.

I have met several individuals who, out of spiritual ideology, gave up all that they owned, moved into the forest to live off the land as ascetics, alone. They came to see me because of certain spiritual issues that were causing havoc in their lives.

To make several long stories short, they were miserable. They believed that by detaching from "the evils of material things," they would be able to live saintly lives in bliss. *Wrong!* Counter to their plan, they were depressed and entirely unable to meditate. They hungered for human interaction; they hungered for everything. They placed themselves in a situation of constant fight with their bodies. Such struggle has nothing to do with unfoldment. In fact, it's quite contrary to unfoldment, because in that struggle there is no clarity.

What went wrong? They were following a template, ignorant of the underlying principle. Effectively they were acting as if they were enlightened, which has nothing to do with actual enlightenment. They had turned themselves into caricatures of sages. Ideology had possessed them to such an extent that they were utterly blind to their folly, despite the full-scale rebellion of their bodies. The suffering recluses had a common question, which went something like this,

"Why do I feel so empty even though I am surrounded by the magnificence of nature?" Instead of exploring that question in their bodies, they usually went back to willfulness.

Masochism, denial, and willfulness fueled by ideology are the causes of their suffering. Quite literally they were punishing themselves in the name of awakening. Isness is not about punishment, is not about suffering. Resistance to what *is* causes suffering. Once we understand how innate conscience guides the unfoldment process, it is wise to put it at the helm of the ship. Any true sage is aware of this truth. Spiritual traditions have largely missed it.

Consider the overwhelming feeling you have when you realize how much needs correcting in your life. All enlightened individuals have had the same realization. They have admitted that they must prune their inner gardens to live inspirience. Otherwise conscience will put up an impenetrable barrier.

Upon realizing the power hidden in conscience and the physical limitations of the human body, if we are being honest, we must admit we can't manage our complicated lives. The next step is to simplify one's life by pruning away the unnecessary. No need to get crazy with the pruners — take some time before you decide to give your house away. Just follow your conscience one step at a time. Quite naturally your life will simplify little by little.

To get started, note the things that require tending to, ask yourself what service those things provide in your life, and then feel into inner space for what to do next. Feel your way through the pruning process without too much thought. How does inner space respond? What does your body want to do?

If you have thoughts like "Someday this will be worth something," or "Someday I will be able to make use of this," remember that your conscience doesn't actually speak in narrative voice. If there is such a voice, consider that it may be rationalization. That said, feel your way through pruning and remain in great appreciation. Take responsibility for what you ultimately do. You have the authority here.

PART 4

Beyond the Self

CHAPTER 15

The Mirrors of Transformation

If you have ever stood between two mirrors, you will have noticed that your reflection appears in both mirrors, queued up to infinity. My childhood home had a bathroom with such mirrors, and I visited it often to glimpse the infinite me-train. Something about that experience kept drawing me back there, day after day, for years. What was it that was drawing me?

Years later, when I opened my own dojo to teach Japanese sword and aikijujutsu, I installed a small wooden Shinto shrine, called a kamidana, on the wall, as is the tradition. A kamidana is a little house with doors, which open to a written prayer that rests within. Before the doors is a mirror, which is the first thing you see when looking at the shrine. Effectively, the first thing you see when you pray is *you.*

Reflecting on Inner Disharmony

Imagine yourself standing at the center of an inwardly mirrored sphere. No matter where you look, images of your body stretch to infinity. Now let's imagine the mirrors are closer, so close that only your face is projected infinitely. Look into your eyes – really look. What do you feel? This experience can be very emotional if taken seriously. If you have trouble imagining, look at an actual mirror up close to see your face clearly. Look deeply, look long. What catches your gaze? What do you feel?

Back to the imaginary mirrored sphere: Remove the physical image entirely and imagine those mirrors reflect your inner space. What would be extended to infinity? If inner space were not clear, we might cringe at the mere thought of that train stretching infinitely.

This mirror analogy is not far from the truth of what is occurring in the world. What is within projects outward, into the world in ways that we are rarely cognizant of. How can we inspirience oneness when we are unconsciously projecting inequity and separation into infinity? Instead of avoiding the inner mirror, let's step right in there and face what we have been avoiding for so long, but do it without a narrative, without condemnation or praise. Observe it; feel it.

By choosing to see the projections, we are now making good use of the observing aspect. You've probably noticed the observing aspect during previous meditation experiences. When the observing aspect comes to the fore, there is sublime silence that observes without condemnation all that is transpiring through and around the body. When the mind rests and the observing aspect becomes primary, the individual has great clarity. What would happen if the observing aspect observed itself in that magic mirror? Try it and see!

Instant global spaciousness is what you get. If you allocated a little time to the infinite mirror, there might be a powerful feeling of vibration within the body. The body loves and responds positively to this frequency. Do this as much as you can throughout your daily life and watch "the walls come crumblin' down," as the song goes.

Social Mirrors

With sufficient inspirience, the perceived duality of the inner and outer dimension begins to fade away, which is to say, the feeling that all is one, there is no other, comes to the fore. Yet despite vast spaciousness, clear conscience, and the penetrating insight that may be our daily inspirience, we may still have trouble interacting with others in ways that allow us to be true to innate conscience without appearing brash.

If we are concerned about our social lives, we may be tempted to compromise truth for conformity. Even small compromises carry big price tags. Unfoldment takes courage, but we don't have to be brash. What if you could interact with people in a way that acknowledged them and revealed their true intentions, without you having to mount a soapbox or compromise integrity? Through such a method, your social interactions with people would bring the observing aspect to the fore within them, thus offering them the opportunity to remove a fold, while keeping egg off your face.

I rarely teach techniques, but this one is so simple anyone could do it, and it serves innate conscience, so I will make an exception. Just be sure that you are observing inner space when using this method.

Imagine that pushy friends are pressuring you to go into business with them, but inner space warns against it. You know they won't take a simple "no" for an answer, but you don't want to hurt their feelings or sever the relationship unnecessarily. The first thing you can do is thank them for considering you. You could say "Wow, I'm honored that you would consider me. Thank you." By saying so, you have acknowledged their acknowledgment of you. Next, you need to turn them down in a way that doesn't automatically sever the relationship or compromise your inner space. You might say, "Do you mind if I go with my intuition on this?" That simple question puts a mirror on the motivations of the questioned person. The vast majority of people, if they respect you at all, will stop pushing and say something like, "Sure, of course," for to do otherwise is to admit that they do not respect your sovereignty as an individual. Then you can simply say that you will have to opt out because it doesn't feel right for your life — full stop.

If they say, "No, you can't do that" or keep pressing in any way, they are openly acknowledging self-centered motivations. They aren't your friends, and they just admitted as much. Give them a flat "No" and be about your life. Unless you are living in a broken culture, very few people will look in the mirror and press on selfishly — that is, behaving as predators.

Unless you like being prey, move on.

Acknowledgment coupled with asking permission is extraordinarily powerful. If you are in a position of authority, instead of barking commands, which tends to strum up feelings of resentment, you can acknowledge a person's situation and then ask permission: "I see you're quite busy, but could I get you to take care of this task I asked you about as soon as possible?" Now, instead of feeling resentment, the individual likely feels that you have taken the time to see him, and that you trust him to get things done. It feels really good to be seen and trusted. Deep down, we all want that. Before you know it, people will be going the extra mile for you because they feel that you have their best interest at heart — be sure that you do.

By simply changing our approach to interactions, we bring the power of consciousness into those interactions. With right speech rooted in spaciousness, the quality of relationships can improve tremendously. If a person looks in the mirror and continues to do the inappropriate, you might save yourself and everyone else a load of frustration by moving forward, without them, unfettered. Many times, just moving forward with your passions changes people for the better, because you are modeling a positive way to live — and that's powerful.

CHAPTER 16

The Transparent Self

One of the unexpected effects of Isness inspirience is the transcendence of belief and ideology. The light of Isness is so clear, penetrating, and complete that assumptions, biases, and beliefs disintegrate. We see clearly that our ideas relating to life, spirituality, religion, and ourselves lack foundation. Isness is like a blazing wildfire of love consuming all that we cling to. How much is consumed is limited only by how long we can stand the flame. Stay in long enough, and even the sense of self evaporates.

After a deep, direct inspirience of Isness, there remains a fresh, new perspective on everything, as if we have been reborn in the world through Isness. The absence of belief can be bewildering at first. Most people believe things based merely upon the confidence, charisma, and popularity of the teacher, not fact or truth. Thus, one effect of Isness inspirience is a loss of confidence in knowledge, belief, bias, and assumption. People equate lack of confidence with weakness, so initially after an Isness inspirience you may seem weak to yourself and others. Only once one realizes that absence of belief is an unshakable foundation does confidence return. People rebut the preceding statement with, "But I am an atheist, so I don't have a belief." But even atheists, if they believe in the self, are utterly immersed in belief. Belief in the self is the first belief system.

If you have successfully paid attention to inner space, you have an inkling of how bound up you are in the self, as is the rest of the world. You see how religions, ideologies, beliefs, philosophies, ideas, biases, assumptions, traumas, habits, and so on are like demons controlling your body as if it were a puppet. Almost all of the thoughts and feelings that you have ever had, even ones of spirituality, have roots in a sense of otherness, of separation, based upon an unquestioned assumption that there is a fixed self, a you.

Suddenly you realize that people resemble zombies, walking around under the spell of self, a dark dream that envelops awareness. Look at anyone whom you have ever known, even the "teachers," and you realize that they are caught up in that dark dream, just as you have been. Almost everything they say and do stems from that dream. You feel a deep sense of compassion for them and wish to help them awaken, to inspirience Isness directly for themselves, but you are entirely ill-equipped for that purpose. Much is required before anyone would ever listen to you in that regard.

The next step is raising yourself anew and maturing into a functional, transparent individual representation of Isness, so that there is no longer the mind-generated unconscious separation of inner and outer dimensions. Instead, Isness will shine through mutable mind-forms that serve functionality in the world. We could call this condition the transparent self. A deep awareness dawns that the name, the body, and so forth are not you, for there is no you. This feeling will remain until some piece of bound self is uncovered, and the zombie arises again to be seen and set aflame by the love of Isness.

Once beliefs have burned away sufficiently, the sense of self is realized to be phantasmal — not ultimately real, yet not entirely false either. The self is kind of like math, in that it's not tangible, for it has no material substance, yet also like math, it has great power. Investment in math leads to technology; investment in the self leads to slavery. Lovingly divesting from the self reveals oneness.

For the awakened individual, the name only identifies the body, much in the way an address identifies a house. We all know that the address is not the same thing as the house. A name allows one body to address another — that is all. A name is not you. Once this realization grows deeper than thought, freedom from the name blossoms, as does lucidity, within the dream of self. Awareness is now able to peek behind the curtain to see the workings of the mind, how it creates the phantom. When we see the mechanism happening in real time within the body, the illusion is irreversibly broken.

Who am I? What am I? These questions arise from the dream, bound in assumption. The awakened one no longer engages these questions, for they give rise to the dreamlike zombie of self — and with the zombie comes suffering.

Let's begin gently seeing through the self. We must go gently, for when the light of Isness shines through the cloud of self, awe results, often followed by suffering that is in direct proportion to the degree of energy bound in the self. Watch the inner narrative and beware of excitement.

Transparent Meditation

The transparent meditation is one of the few meditations that I advise be done initially while lying down. We may be transcending the limits of proprioception, which is your sense of how your body is positioned in space. If this sense goes awry while you're standing, the result could be dangerous. Proprioception is a mental and sensory model of your body. To get an idea of what proprioception is, while standing, close your eyes, extend your right hand out ninety degrees and extend your pointer finger. With your eyes still closed, touch the very tip of your nose with the tip of your pointer finger. You may notice while doing this exercise that you have some sort of mental image of where your arm and your face are in space relative to each other. This imagery allows you to have functional movement in the world. Most people miss their noses more than 50 percent of the time on initial attempts, but proprioception can be improved through training.

For most people, the mental image and feeling of the body are tightly defined, creating a powerful sense of separation from all that is around the body. This meditation is going to make the delineation of your model of the body more transparent, so that the sense of oneness can come to the fore. Counterintuitively, doing this meditation will improve proprioception.

In our initial experiences of the transparent meditation, I recommend that you cover your body with a blanket, for your blood pressure may lower significantly, causing your body temperature to drop and resulting in a distracting chill.

We want to begin this meditation in as innocent a state as possible, so, as much as possible, set aside all expectation and assumption, for they can only block your process. Initially, allocate at least a half hour for this meditation. An hour would be better. Two hours — gold. Lie down comfortably and close your eyes. If lying down is impossible, just choose the most comfortable position that you can.

In the transparent meditation we will be working with our mental and sensory image of the body, our proprioception. We will be moving toward a lighter, more expansive, more transparent inner space. To make progress we must begin to "see through" the image of the body. We will not concern ourselves with external stimuli like the ticking of the clock or the particulars of the external world around us. Accept all that is external and move forward with your meditation.

Note: If at any time during this meditation your body feels achy and needs to be moved, just allow the physical adjustment to occur in the background of your awareness. Keep the meditation process primary.

Begin relaxing more and more deeply as you expand inner space spherically. As inner space expands, intend that your bodily sense becomes lighter and more transparent. As the spaciousness expands and the sense of the body gradually disappears, include all that *is* into your meditation so that the entire universe somehow feels lighter and more transparent. By doing so you are setting aside your habitual sense of separation from all that is.

Keep lightly extending until you feel something is blocking the process. Ask what it is that is blocking while you feel for any disharmony, thoughts, or emotions. Probably there is much negativity to let go, to forgive. But each person is unique, so just go with what you discover without expectation. If you are unable to identify the exact nature of a particular disharmony, do not be concerned. Just feel into the location and general nature of the disturbance, then make it lighter and more transparent until it fades away. You will notice as you progress in this meditation that your breath tends to get softer and softer. This is normal.

Resume the expansion process with your ever-softening breath until you hit another blockage, then investigate and lighten and release it. As you progress, the things that catch your attention will tend to grow smaller and smaller. No matter how small and seemingly insignificant they are, release them. Just keep moving forward. You may reach a point at which you are no longer even sure your body is breathing. You might wonder if it has died — it hasn't.

In my case, I was in this meditation for several hours before I consciously recognized the presence of Isness. As I was trying to transcend the pain of a broken ankle, I wasn't concerned about time. I had little choice but to meditate. I had to "disappear," get lighter, to transcend the pain. Although the pain never fully left, it diminished into the distant background, a bodily experience behind inspirience.

You may want to set aside a large chunk of time to go deep into this meditation, but if time is limited, just go as deeply as you can with the time that you have available. Most importantly, toss all expectations, for expectation is an impenetrable wall. Enter this meditation as purely as you can to smooth out inner space, reduce your sense of separation, and release blockages. Enjoy it.

When the meditation is over, take note of the blockages that you experienced, especially the ones for which action is required, and do something about them. Taking responsibility is what brings inspirience beyond meditation and into daily life. To do so is to live in inspirience.

The Nature of Isness

It is tempting to say that Isness is what *is*, and that sounds quite reasonable, but if we take a look back at the previous sentence, we find a fundamental flaw that indicates bound perception. We have defined Isness as being what *is*, which is to limit Isness to existence. The truth of Isness is entirely beyond the capacity of the mind or words to describe. Even to say that it *is*, is incorrect. It *is*, *is not*, *is both* and *is neither* simultaneously — and even *that* statement is false.

Our "perception" of Isness is limited by the depth of inspirience. At a shallow level, Isness is just what *is*, which is to say, it is exactly the experience of life in the moment. It is just immediacy and aliveness. At such a level, there is no perceived "intelligence" to Isness, no instructive element. Further into inspirience, immediacy leads to transparency, which leads to vibrant total presence — the sense of oneness, which may lead to vibrant total intelligence. Once perception has reached vibrant total intelligence, there can be deep communication and learning.

Many teachings of nonduality stop at immediacy, and thus disregard anything more as being illusory, nonsensical. But the reality is that even immediacy is beyond words. Even to say that this moment *is*, is false. To say that it *is not* is equally false. To limit the transcendent according to words and finite human perception is an attempt to encapsulate, to define — a trap of the self. Even "all is one, there is no other," although helpful in unbinding the self, is a limitation that is ultimately transcended. What remains?

CHAPTER 17

The Master

The birth of self is the birth of deceit, for only when there exists the sense of self and the sense of other does the possibility of deceit arise. Yet the possibility of deceit gives birth to virtue, for only when deceit is truly seen from within and transcended can there be wisdom. Here is the meaning of self-mastery. No matter who you are or what you have done, self-mastery is a possibility.

There was a place, undefined, unbound, clear, and blissful. In this place there was support and repose. There was no sense of self or other in this place. There was no fear, anger, resentment, envy, or suffering of any kind. There was only the undifferentiated moment of bliss.

Then began strange vibrations, tensions, movements, followed by scents and tastes, vague, distant and unfamiliar at first, but ever more intense, stimulating, captivating. Sounds followed, some comforting and others disturbing. Then there were vague shades of light and darkness. All these stimuli were in the background of undifferentiated being until they gradually moved to the fore.

Then came intense pressure, followed by cold, hunger, thirst. Undifferentiated being was then in the background, easily disturbed by these unbidden senses. Suckling, crying, and smiling followed the senses. Blurry images appeared, arms moved, fingers gripped. Myriad feelings arose, some agreeable and others disagreeable. The sounds "Mommy" and "Daddy" were comforting, pleasurable, and stimulating.

Little by little grew the understanding of the body, relative to other. And with this understanding, the body began to navigate other. A feeling of control grew within as "your" desire seemed to guide some movements. Other times the body seemed to move on its own.

There was a sound — your name — associated with the body, and the more it was heard and recognized, the more *you* were there. Then the feeling that *you* were the experience became constant. You knew that you liked and disliked things, and you chose among them. Then you could articulate those opinions, which helped you to get what you wanted and avoid what you didn't want. You could say "I am me."

Little by little you got to know your strengths and weaknesses, your proclivities, and your place in the external world. You developed opinions about yourself, others, and the world. Feelings, thoughts, and words swarmed to reinforce your belief in the self until it appeared perfectly real.

The mental voice reinforced "you"; for example, you ate peas and found the taste repulsive, so the inner voice said, "I hate peas." As you grew, your sense of self was modified by your parents, neighbors, friends, school, ethnicity, culture, talents, knowledge, career, college, and the greater society. All of these things served to make you who you were, both the strengths and the limitations.

Interest in spirituality began, and you were drawn to the idea of awakening. As unfoldment progressed you began to realize that very little of what you believed to be you was necessary for functionality, and much of it was harmful. As unfoldment progressed further still, the self was no longer seen as a truth. Over time, the sense of "you" began to thin. At some point, the self was nothing more than the address label on the body, allowing for communication with other bodies. "Your" memories were no longer identified as being you, so little by little memories ceased to torment you through feelings of nostalgia and regret. Instead, they primarily served the process of unfoldment and functionality in the world.

Now you are largely free of the suffering of memory.

From here, anything that is out of alignment with Isness, that does not serve, is questioned and explored. Biases and assumptions are weaned of the unconscious energy that "you" used to feed them through belief and reactivity, and as they lose energy, peace is revealed. This is the re-raising of the individual through Isness.

As the self thins further, a sense of transparency emerges, as if the sense of self was somehow clear, and the long-lost sense of undifferentiated being gradually returns. The individual has come full circle. So goes the soul, from unconscious oneness to self-conscious slavery, on to oneness through the transparent self — a body now free of the dream of separation.

The ancient Buddhists would indicate that awakened body as the Buddha. The Taoists might call her the Master. And the early Christians might say he is the Christ. But the awakened one never believes such labels, for she understands that naming is the origin of particular things, not of the eternally real. Thus, through the transparent self, Isness expresses consciously into the world. The Master is here.

So you see, the body is the temple. The mind, the self, and experience are the perfect path leading full circle to the origin, the wellspring of life that has been awaiting revelation into the world. And once all the folds of self have been removed, leaving only that which serves transparently, then and only then does Isness flow unhindered through the body.

Now you see that the perfection you long sought was within, and each stone blocking the path was the next step forward in the circle to a functional oneness. The dark dream of self that enslaved the mind is no more. The mind now serves as the divine tool of Isness to shine into the world of existence. Inspirience and experience are now one and the same, and all that was ever felt, thought, said, or done in inequity is seen to be exactly what was needed for the mind/body's reunification through pure being. One recognizes that there are no accidents in the great mystery, yet one doesn't try to understand how that is so, for to define is to confine, to limit, and to dive back into unconscious slavery.

In your process of unfoldment, you have been given much, and as Jesus said, "For everyone to whom much is given, from him much will be required; and to whom much has been committed, of him they will ask the more." Now is the time to be of service in the world by rectifying your life through global appreciation, innate conscience, unconditioned awareness, and the transparent self — ultimately, Isness. As the volume of conscience rises and the inner space broadens, true confidence and ability to see the self and others are unbound, as is the capacity to honestly acknowledge what is happening within the inner spaciousness, as well as with others, to see all situations without condemnation or pity, to listen and to speak in ways that support unfoldment.

Your life is like a flame that lights the candles of seekers. Individuals who fear the light will naturally distance themselves. Let them go. Your job is not to save them, but instead to remain clear and allow the light to do the rest. As "you" become more transparent, the field of integrity grows larger and larger around you as it spreads from person to person, and, little by little, those people who were initially afraid of transparency begin to warm to it.

Now you sit at the nexus point between form and formlessness, the finite and infinite, the one and the many. All that *is* is within you, and you are within it. There is a presence, intelligence, and power so perfect, so loving that no human words can adequately describe it, and it's you.

Now is the time to purify inner space, to boldly face that which has been causing suffering, to take full responsibility for your life, and in doing so, end the slavery of the mind. Thus, the demon of self becomes an angel in service; the body becomes the beacon of light to the world. All is one, there is no other.

Do you have something better to do with your time?

Many Blessings,
Richard L. Haight

If you enjoyed reading Inspirience, please leave a review at your favorite online vendor. Thank you!

Dear reader, you are also invited to a bonus 13-part audio series "Taking Spiritual Authority in Daily Life" by Richard L. Haight.

www.richardhaight.net

Acknowledgments

In memory of Michiko Suga (Sep 4th, 1959 - Sep 14, 2017)

First, my humble and heartfelt appreciation goes to my martial arts instructor Shizen Osaki, who set aside a tremendous amount of time to help me explore this path of spiritual unfoldment.

To my copy-editor, Ed Hall of Hallworks Productions, and to my proofreader, Hester Lee Furey, I extend my most sincere appreciation.

To Justin Hager, Kris Kokay, Celina Reppond, Lennon Pierce, Nichole Owens, Jean Adrienne, Billy Atwell, and William Arsenis, I give my thanks for their early feedback on the manuscript.

I'd like to thank my wife, Teruko Haight, the wind beneath my wings.

Self-publishing is an expensive enterprise, and I have been blessed with the support of many generous individuals whose donations have allowed for publishing. As a way of showing my appreciation for those generous donors, I list their names here:

Diane Ferdig, Todd Nelson, Jason "JJ" Wu, Kathryn Reppond, Gordon Haight, Jim Posner, Ahmet Aral, Anna Salenius, Steve Wieck, Jean Holley, Tom Geissinger

Thank you all for sharing your hard-earned energy in order to assist in the publishing of this work.

Glossary

Cultural Conscience   the conscience that helps individuals fit into society.

Deceit   the quality of being dishonest or misleading. Any action or inaction, which includes thoughts and feelings born of the sense of otherness.

Differentiated   to become distinct or different in character.

Experience   the act or process of directly perceiving events or reality.

Innate Conscience   a form of conscience that is born of a sense of connection to all that is.

Inspirience   a transcended or unconditioned experience. The root terms of inspirience are inspire and experience.

Isness   the most fundamental foundation of all that is. Formless yet throughout all form. Soul and Isness are interchangeable terms indicating the same thing.

Learned Conscience   what one has been taught with regard to being correct, right, or morally good.

Neuroplasticity   the capacity of the brain to develop

and change throughout life.

Self the union of elements (such as body, emotions, thoughts, and sensations) that constitute the individuality and identity of a person.

Soul the most fundamental foundation of all that is. Formless yet throughout all form. Soul and Isness are interchangeable terms indicating the same thing.

Transparent Self a body now free of the dream of separation.

Unbinding the process of releasing the structures of self that have veiled or bound the soul.

Unconditioned Love a love that springs from direct inspirience with Isness. Unconditioned love is not a mood, ideology, philosophy, or belief.

Unconditioned Meditation a meditation that is free of form.

Undifferentiated not divided into different elements, types, etc.

Unfoldment the process of undoing the sense of self to discover Isness within.

Appendix

Unconditioned Meditation
Eyes: Open
Position: Initially seated
Duration: At least 15 minutes initially

Open the senses spherically, beginning with sight and continuing in steps through sound, smell, taste, and finally the feeling of the body. Relax as much as possible and gradually incorporate movement and other daily life challenges into this meditation.

Appreciation Meditation
Eyes: Open
Position: Meditator's choice
Time duration: At least 15 minutes initially

Start with spherical awareness as practiced in unconditioned meditation. Think of something for which you have a pure appreciation. Feel where that appreciation is located in the body. Remember the feeling and let go the image. Expand the feeling of pure appreciation throughout the body evenly, without forcing it. Finally, share appreciation globally.

Flash Meditation
Eyes: Open
Position: Meditator's choice
Time duration: A few seconds

Take a moment to notice your inner turmoil. Then instantly meditate calm, global appreciation. Continue with your day in appreciation for as long as it lasts. Use a clock or some regularly recurring event as a reminder to flash meditate throughout the day.

Conscience Meditation
Eyes: Open
Position: Meditator's choice
Time duration: At least 20 minutes initially

Notice the size and degree of inner spaciousness. Expand the feeling of spaciousness globally to the entire universe. Relax into this process and enjoy it. Use this meditation to correct your life. Correct small things first, then gradually work your way up to larger issues.

Reordering Meditation
Eyes: Open
Position: Meditator's choice
Duration: As long as it takes

Notice a place that is calling out to you to tidy up. Expand inner spaciousness universally. Tune to unconditioned appreciation. Allow the intensity of appreciation to build around you. Notice what catches your eye. Feel where the body wants to go. Feel how things wish to be rearranged. Release the reins of your body and allow it to do the work. Enjoy the show.

Mirror Meditation
Eyes: Open or closed
Position: Meditator's choice
Duration: As long as it takes

Imagine yourself standing at the center of a spherical, inwardly reflecting mirror. Examine your face and feel into any disharmony there. Remove the image of physical self and allow the content of the mind to reflect via the spherical mirror. Feel what would naturally reflect to the universe — the good, the bad, and the ugly. Finally set aside the content of the self and allow what remains to reflect in the mirror universally.

Transparent Meditation
Eyes: Closed initially
Position: Lying down or some other comfortable position
Duration: 30 minutes to 2 hours

Consider using a blanket to cover the body and prevent its temperature from dropping too much. Have no expectation for results. Just enjoy the process. Relax ever deeper while expanding inner space globally. Allow the perception of the body to gradually become more transparent, and eventually to disappear. Scan spaciousness for anything that hooks attention or blocks progress in this meditation. Intend the blockage to become lighter and more transparent until it vanishes. Keep moving forward

Notes

Biblical References taken from the New King James Version®. Copyright © 1982 by Thomas Nelson. Used by permission. All rights reserved.

About the Author

Richard L. Haight is an instructor of martial, meditation and healing arts, and he is the author of *The Unbound Soul: A Spiritual Memoir for Personal Transformation and Enlightenment.*

He began his path of awakening at age eight when he made a solemn promise in a vision to dedicate his life to enlightenment and to share what he found with the world. He took his first steps towards that promise at age 12 when he began formal martial arts training.

At the age of 24, Richard moved to Japan to advance his training with masters of the sword, staff, and aiki-jujutsu. During his 15 years living in Japan, Richard was awarded masters licenses in four samurai arts as well as a traditional healing art called Sotai-ho.

Throughout his life, Richard has had a series of profound visions that have ultimately guided him to the realization of the Oneness that the ancient spiritual teachers often spoke of. This understanding ultimately transformed the arts that he teaches and has resulted in the writing of *The Unbound Soul.*

Through his books, his meditation and martial arts seminar, Richard Haight is helping to ignite a worldwide spiritual awakening that is free of all constraints and open to anyone of any level. Richard Haight now lives and teaches in southern Oregon, U.S.A.

Richard Haight explains that true spiritual enlightenment embraces all of life with deep aliveness, authenticity, innocence and authority. It is what you are truly seeking.

The Unbound Soul

*A Spiritual Memoir for Personal
Transformation and Enlightenment*

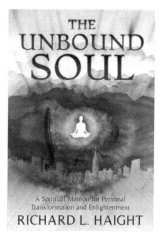

The heartfelt, true story of a young boy, who, in the midst of a vision, dedicates his life to spiritual awakening. As he matures into a man, this promise leads him across the globe, gathering ancient knowledge and mastering martial, healing, and meditation arts. Along the way, subsequent visions reveal the rapidly approaching collapse that will shake our societies, our economic system, and the earth's ecology to the very core. Tormented by visions of coming worldwide calamity, he presses ever onward in his search and eventually realizes the elusive truth hinted at in his childhood vision. In *The Unbound Soul*, Haight reveals the profoundly simple yet elusive truth that illuminates your life. *The Unbound Soul* is really about you and your path toward practical realization in everyday life.

The Psychedelic Path

*An Exploration of Shamanic Plants
for Spiritual Awakening*

Are you curious about psychedelics? Learn the potential benefits and dangers of taking hallucinogens through the author's deep exploration and the most current scientific studies.

Richard L. Haight, bestselling author of *The Unbound Soul* provides a powerful, intimate, unbiased account of hallucinogens as they relate to the spiritual path.

"This book is a page-turner, exciting, and written with captivating imagery that transports you on this psychedelic journey."

For his journeys, Haight makes use of three ancient shamanic plants found in South, Central, and North America, and he discovers a fresh perspective that catalyzes tremendous personal transformation.

The Psychedelic Path is a book for you if:

- You are serious about spiritual awakening but are unsure whether psychedelics are right for you
- You are frightened by the prospect of "bad trips" but still feel pulled to psychedelics
- You already employ psychedelics but are looking for a fresh, more powerful approach
- You want to confront your own deepest, oldest inner demons, but you're having trouble "getting there"
- You want to live a life filled with love and courage, beyond all excuses

"I felt elation and had the sense I was taking part in an epic or classic fairy tale—the quest, fighting the dragons and the final hard-won conquest."

"It's time for the stigma to be lifted from our sacred plant teachers! This book is definitely a step in that direction."

"If you find yourself with an opportunity to take another trip, do yourself a favor and read The Psychedelic Path first."